Cram101 Textbook Outlines to accompany:

Interplay: The Process of Interpersonal Communication

Adler, Rosenfeld & Proctor, 10th Edition

A Content Technologies Inc. publication (c) 2012.

Learning System

Cram101 Textbook Outlines is a learning system. The notes in this book are the highlights of your textbook, you will never have to highlight a book again.

How to use this book. Take this book to class, it is your notebook for the lecture. The notes and highlights on the left hand side of the pages follow the outline and order of the textbook. All you have to do is follow along while your instructor presents the lecture. Circle the items emphasized in class and add other important information on the right side. With Cram101 Textbook Outlines you'll spend less time writing and more time listening. Learning becomes more efficient.

Cram101.com Online

Increase your studying efficiency by using Cram101.com's practice tests and online reference material. It is the perfect complement to Cram101 Textbook Outlines. Use self-teaching matching tests or simulate in-class testing with comprehensive multiple choice tests, or simply use Cram's true and false tests for quick review. Cram101.com even allows you to enter your in-class notes for an integrated studying format combining the textbook notes with your class notes.

Visit **www.Cram101.com**, click Sign Up at the top of the screen, and enter **DK73DW4073** in the promo code box on the registration screen. Your access to www.Cram101.com is discounted by 50% because you have purchased this book. Sign up and stop highlighting textbooks forever.

Interplay: The Process of Interpersonal Communication
Adler, Rosenfeld & Proctor, 10th

CONTENTS

Chapter 1. Interpersonal Process

Computer-mediated communication	Computer-mediated communication is defined as any communicative transaction that occurs through the use of two or more networked computers. While the term has traditionally referred to those communications that occur via computer-mediated formats (e.g., instant messages, e-mails, chat rooms), it has also been applied to other forms of text-based interaction such as text messaging. Research on Computer mediated communication focuses largely on the social effects of different computer-supported communication technologies.
Interpersonal communication	Interpersonal communication is usually defined by communication scholars in numerous ways, usually describing participants who are dependent upon one another and have a shared history. It can involve one on one conversations or individuals interacting with many people within a society. It helps us understand how and why people behave and communicate in different ways to construct and negotiate a social reality.
Emperor	An emperor is a (male) monarch, usually the sovereign ruler of an empire or another type of imperial realm. Empress, the female equivalent, may indicate an emperor's wife (empress consort) or a woman who rules in her own right (empress regnant). Emperors are generally recognized to be of a higher honor and rank than kings.
Michelangelo	The Michelangelo virus is a computer virus first discovered in April 1991 in New Zealand. The virus was designed to infect DOS systems (but did not engage the operating system or make any OS calls; Michelangelo, like all boot sector viruses, basically operated at the BIOS level) and remained dormant until March 6, the birthday of Renaissance artist Michelangelo. There is no reference to the artist in the virus, and it is doubtful that the virus writer intended Michelangelo to be referenced to the virus.
Space	Space is the boundless, three-dimensional extent in which objects and events occur and have relative position and direction. Physical space is often conceived in three linear dimensions, although modern physicists usually consider it, with time, to be part of the boundless four-dimensional continuum known as spacetime. In mathematics one examines 'spaces' with different numbers of dimensions and with different underlying structures.
Bridge	A bridge is a type of social tie that connects two different groups in a social network. General Bridge In general, a bridge is a direct tie between nodes that would otherwise be in disconnected components of the graph.

Chapter 1. Interpersonal Process

This means that say that A and B make up a social networking graph, n_1 is in A, n_2 is in B, and there is a social tie e between n_1 and n_2.

Genie	Genie is the pseudonym for a feral child who spent nearly all of the first thirteen years of her life locked inside a bedroom strapped to a potty chair. She was a victim of one of the most severe cases of social isolation in American history. Genie was discovered by Los Angeles authorities on November 4, 1970.
Death	Death is the termination of the biological functions that sustain a living organism. The word refers both to the particular processes of life's cessation as well as to the condition or state of a formerly living body. Phenomena which commonly bring about death include predation, malnutrition, accidents resulting in terminal injury, and disease.
Identity	Identity is an umbrella term used throughout the social sciences to describe a person's conception and expression of their individuality or group affiliations (such as national identity and cultural identity). The term is used more specifically in psychology and sociology, including the two forms of social psychology. The term is also used with respect to place identity.
First date	A first date is any type of initial meeting between two individuals whether or not previously acquainted where an effort is made to ask, plan and organize some sort of social activity. Dating can vary between cultures, lifestyles, religion, gender, and sexual orientation. In many countries and cultures it is the process that romantic relationships are developed and future spouses are found.
Publics	Publics are small groups of people who follow one or more particular issue very closely. They are well informed about the issue(s) and also have a very strong opinion on it/them. They tend to know more about politics than the average person, and, therefore, exert more influence, because these people care so deeply about their cause(s) that they donate much time and money.
Conflict resolution	Conflict resolution is a range of methods of eliminating sources of conflict. The term 'conflict resolution' is sometimes used interchangeably with the term dispute resolution or alternative dispute resolution. Processes of conflict resolution generally include negotiation, mediation, and diplomacy.

Clam101

Chapter 1. Interpersonal Process

Resolution	A resolution is a written motion adopted by a deliberative body. The substance of the resolution can be anything that can normally be proposed as a motion. For long or important motions, though, it is often better to have them written out so that discussion is easier or so that it can be distributed outside of the body after its adoption.
Self-actualization	Self-actualization is a term that has been used in various psychology theories, often in slightly different ways. The term was originally introduced by the organismic theorist Kurt Goldstein for the motive to realize one's full potential. In his view, it is the organism's master motive, the only real motive: 'the tendency to actualize itself as fully as possible is the basic drive...the drive of self-actualization'.
Self-esteem	Self-esteem is a term used in psychology to reflect a person's overall evaluation or appraisal of his or her own worth. Self-esteem encompasses beliefs (for example, 'I am competent', 'I am worthy') and emotions such as triumph, despair, pride and shame. Self-esteem can apply specifically to a particular dimension (for example, 'I believe I am a good writer and I feel happy about that') or have global extent (for example, 'I believe I am a bad person, and feel bad of myself in general').
Environment	The biophysical environment is the symbiosis between the physical environment and the biological life forms within the environment, and includes all variables that comprise the Earth's biosphere. The biophysical environment can be divided into two categories: the natural environment and the built environment, with some overlap between the two. Following the industrial revolution, the built environment has become an increasingly significant part of the Earth's environment.
Interaction	In statistics, an interaction may arise when considering the relationship among three or more variables, and describes a situation in which the simultaneous influence of two variables on a third is not additive. Most commonly, interactions are considered in the context of regression analyses.

The presence of interactions can have important implications for the interpretation of statistical models. |

CYam\101

Chapter 1. Interpersonal Process

Family	In human context, a family is a group of people affiliated by consanguinity, affinity, or co-residence. In most societies it is the principal institution for the socialization of children. Extended from the human 'family unit' by biological-cultural affinity, marriage, economy, culture, tradition, honor, and friendship are concepts of family that are physical and metaphorical, or that grow increasingly inclusive extending to community, village, city, region, nationhood, global village and humanism.
Nonverbal communication	Nonverbal communication is usually understood as the process of communication through sending and receiving wordless messages. i.e., language is not the only source of communication, there are other means also. Messages can be communicated through gestures and touch (Haptic communication), by body language or posture, by facial expression and eye contact.
Dyad	A dyad in sociology is a noun used to describe a group of two people. 'Dyadic' is an adjective used to describe this type of communication/interaction. A dyad is the smallest possible social group.
Language	Language may refer either to the specifically human capacity for acquiring and using complex systems of communication, or to a specific instance of such a system of complex communication. The scientific study of language in any of its senses is called linguistics. The approximately 3000-6000 languages that are spoken by humans today are the most salient examples, but natural languages can also be based on visual rather than auditive stimuli, for example in sign languages and written language.
Skill	A skill is the learned capacity to carry out pre-determined results often with the minimum outlay of time, energy, or both. Skills can often be divided into domain-general and domain-specific skills. For example, in the domain of work, some general skills would include time management, teamwork and leadership, self motivation and others, whereas domain-specific skills would be useful only for a certain job.
Interdependence	**Interdependence is a dynamic of being mutually and physically responsible to, and sharing a common set of principles with, others. This concept differs distinctly from 'dependence,' which implies that each member of a relationship cannot function or survive apart from one another. In an interdependent relationship, all participants are emotionally, economically, ecologically and/or morally self-reliant while at the same time responsible to each other.**

CLAM101

Chapter 1. Interpersonal Process

Self-disclosure	Self-disclosure is both the conscious and unconscious act of revealing more about oneself to others. This may include, but is not limited to, thoughts, feelings, aspirations, goals, failures, successes, fears, dreams as well as one's likes, dislikes, and favorites.
	Typically, a self-disclosure happens when we initially meet someone and continues as we build and develop our relationships with people.
Webcam	A webcam is a video camera which feeds its images in real time to a computer or computer network, often via USB, ethernet or Wi-Fi.
	Their most popular use is the establishment of video links, permitting computers to act as videophones or videoconference stations. This common use as a video camera for the World Wide Web gave the webcam its name.
Erin Brockovich	Erin Brockovich is a 2000 drama film which dramatizes the story of Erin Brockovich's legal fight against the US West Coast energy corporation Pacific Gas and Electric Company (PG'E). The film was directed by Steven Soderbergh and starred Julia Roberts, who won the Academy Award, Golden Globe, Screen Actors' Guild Award and BAFTA for Best Actress. It is based on a true story, and the real Erin Brockovich has a cameo appearance as a waitress named Julia.
Cognitive complexity	Cognitive complexity describes cognition along a simplicity-complexity axis. It is the subject of academic study in fields including personal construct psychology, organisational theory and human-computer interaction.
	History
	First proposed by James Bieri in 1955.

Chapter 1. Interpersonal Process

Empathy	Empathy is the capacity to recognize and, to some extent, share feelings (such as sadness or happiness) that are being experienced by another semi-sentient being. Someone may need to have a certain amount of empathy before they are able to feel compassion. Etymology The English word is derived from the Greek word ?μπ?θεια (empatheia), 'physical affection, passion, partiality' which comes from ?v (en), 'in, at' + π?θος (pathos), 'passion' or 'suffering'.
Perspective	Perspective in pharmacoeconomics refers to the economic vantage point that is being taken in a pharmacoeconomic analysis, such as a cost-effectiveness analysis or cost-utility analysis. This will affect the types of costs (resource expenditures) and benefits that will be considered relevant to the analysis. Five general perspectives that are often cited in pharmacoeconomics include: institutional, third party, patient, governmental and societal.

Chapter 2. Culture and Communication

Genie	Genie is the pseudonym for a feral child who spent nearly all of the first thirteen years of her life locked inside a bedroom strapped to a potty chair. She was a victim of one of the most severe cases of social isolation in American history. Genie was discovered by Los Angeles authorities on November 4, 1970.
Space	Space is the boundless, three-dimensional extent in which objects and events occur and have relative position and direction. Physical space is often conceived in three linear dimensions, although modern physicists usually consider it, with time, to be part of the boundless four-dimensional continuum known as spacetime. In mathematics one examines 'spaces' with different numbers of dimensions and with different underlying structures.
Global village	Global Village is a term closely associated with Marshall McLuhan, popularized in his books The Gutenberg Galaxy: The Making of Typographic Man (1962) and Understanding Media (1964). McLuhan described how the globe has been contracted into a village by electric technology and the instantaneous movement of information from every quarter to every point at the same time. In bringing all social and political functions together in a sudden implosion, electric speed heightened human awareness of responsibility to an intense degree.
Interaction	In statistics, an interaction may arise when considering the relationship among three or more variables, and describes a situation in which the simultaneous influence of two variables on a third is not additive. Most commonly, interactions are considered in the context of regression analyses. The presence of interactions can have important implications for the interpretation of statistical models.
Group	In the social sciences a group can be defined as two or more humans who interact with one another, accept expectations and obligations as members of the group, and share a common identity. By this definition, society can be viewed as a large group, though most social groups are considerably smaller. A true group exhibits some degree of social cohesion and is more than a simple collection or aggregate of individuals, such as people waiting at a bus stop.

Chapter 2. Culture and Communication

Intercultural communication	Intercultural communication is a form of global communication. It is used to describe the wide range of communication problems that naturally appear within an organization made up of individuals from different religious, social, ethnic, and educational backgrounds. Intercultural communication is sometimes used synonymously with cross-cultural communication.
Out-group	In sociology, an out-group is a social group towards which an individual feels contempt, opposition, or a desire to compete. Members of outgroups may be subject to outgroup homogeneity biases, and generally people tend to privilege ingroup members over outgroup members in many situations. The term originates from social identity theory.
Computer-mediated communication	Computer-mediated communication is defined as any communicative transaction that occurs through the use of two or more networked computers. While the term has traditionally referred to those communications that occur via computer-mediated formats (e.g., instant messages, e-mails, chat rooms), it has also been applied to other forms of text-based interaction such as text messaging. Research on Computer mediated communication focuses largely on the social effects of different computer-supported communication technologies.
Interpersonal communication	Interpersonal communication is usually defined by communication scholars in numerous ways, usually describing participants who are dependent upon one another and have a shared history. It can involve one on one conversations or individuals interacting with many people within a society. It helps us understand how and why people behave and communicate in different ways to construct and negotiate a social reality.
Norm	Social norms are the behaviors and cues within a society or group. This sociological term has been defined as 'the rules that a group uses for appropriate and inappropriate values, beliefs, attitudes and behaviors. These rules may be explicit or implicit.
Publics	Publics are small groups of people who follow one or more particular issue very closely. They are well informed about the issue(s) and also have a very strong opinion on it/them. They tend to know more about politics than the average person, and, therefore, exert more influence, because these people care so deeply about their cause(s) that they donate much time and money.
Power	In physics, power is the rate at which work is performed or energy is converted As a simple example, if an elevated reservoir is used to drive a waterwheel, then replacing its drain valve with another of larger diameter does not change the water's potential energy, but does increase the available power because the larger valve allows higher flow, so the potential energy can be more quickly converted into kinetic energy.

CRAM101

If ΔW is the amount of work performed during a period of time of duration Δt, the average power P_{avg} over that period is given by the formula

$$P_{avg} = \frac{\Delta W}{\Delta t} .$$

It is the average amount of work done or energy converted per unit of time. The average power is often simply called 'power' when the context makes it clear.

Index

In computer science, an index can be:

1. an integer which identifies an array element
2. a data structure that enables sublinear-time lookup

Array element identifier

When data objects are stored in an array, individual objects are selected by an index which is usually a non-negative scalar integer. Indices are also called subscripts.

There are three ways in which the elements of an array can be indexed:

0 (zero-based indexing)
  The first element of the array is indexed by subscript of 0.
1 (one-based indexing)
  The first element of the array is indexed by subscript of 1.
n (n-based indexing)
  The base index of an array can be freely chosen.

Chapter 2. Culture and Communication

Achievement	An achievement is entitled. It can include not only the coat of arms itself, but also: the crest; a torse; mantling; the appropriate helm, coronet or crown; the supporters (who may or may not be depicted on a compartment); the motto; and in some cases the symbol of an order.
Family	In human context, a family is a group of people affiliated by consanguinity, affinity, or co-residence. In most societies it is the principal institution for the socialization of children. Extended from the human 'family unit' by biological-cultural affinity, marriage, economy, culture, tradition, honor, and friendship are concepts of family that are physical and metaphorical, or that grow increasingly inclusive extending to community, village, city, region, nationhood, global village and humanism.
Identity	Identity is an umbrella term used throughout the social sciences to describe a person's conception and expression of their individuality or group affiliations (such as national identity and cultural identity). The term is used more specifically in psychology and sociology, including the two forms of social psychology. The term is also used with respect to place identity.
Language	Language may refer either to the specifically human capacity for acquiring and using complex systems of communication, or to a specific instance of such a system of complex communication. The scientific study of language in any of its senses is called linguistics. The approximately 3000-6000 languages that are spoken by humans today are the most salient examples, but natural languages can also be based on visual rather than auditive stimuli, for example in sign languages and written language.
College	A college is an educational institution or a constituent part of an educational institution. Usage varies in English-speaking nations. A college may be a degree-awarding tertiary educational institution, an institution within a federal university, an institution offering vocational education, or a secondary school.
Student	A student is a learner, or someone who attends an educational institution. In some nations, the English term (or its cognate in another language) is reserved for those who attend university, while a schoolchild under the age of eighteen is called a pupil in English (or an equivalent in other languages). In its widest use, student is used for anyone who is learning.

Chapter 2. Culture and Communication

Wedding	A wedding is the ceremony in which two people are united in marriage or a similar institution. Wedding traditions and customs vary greatly between cultures, ethnic groups, religions, countries, and social classes. Most wedding ceremonies involve an exchange of wedding vows by the couple, presentation of a gift (offering, ring(s), symbolic item, flowers, money), and a public proclamation of marriage by an authority figure or leader.
Contact	In family law, contact is one of the general terms which denotes the level of contact a parent or other significant person in a child's life can have with that child. Contact forms part of the bundle of rights and privileges which a parent may have in relation to any child of the family. Following ratification of the United Nations Convention on the Rights of the Child in most countries, the term 'access' was superseded by the term contact.
Eye contact	Eye contact is a meeting of the eyes between two individuals. In human beings, eye contact is a form of nonverbal communication and is thought to have a large influence on social behavior. Coined in the early to mid-1960s, the term has come in the West to often define the act as a meaningful and important sign of confidence and social communication.
Personal space	Personal space is the region surrounding a person which they regard as psychologically theirs. Invasion of personal space often leads to discomfort, anger, or anxiety on the part of the victim. The notion of personal space comes from Edward T. Hall, whose ideas were influenced by Heini Hediger's studies of behavior of zoo animals.
Attribution	Attribution is a concept in social psychology referring to how individuals explain causes of behavior and events. Attribution theory is an umbrella term for various theories that attempt to explain these processes. Fritz Heider first proposed a theory of attribution The Psychology of Interpersonal Relations.
Dialect	The term dialect is used in two distinct ways, even by linguists. One usage refers to a variety of a language that is a characteristic of a particular group of the language's speakers. The term is applied most often to regional speech patterns, but a dialect may also be defined by other factors, such as social class.

Chapter 2. Culture and Communication

Conflict resolution	Conflict resolution is a range of methods of eliminating sources of conflict. The term 'conflict resolution' is sometimes used interchangeably with the term dispute resolution or alternative dispute resolution. Processes of conflict resolution generally include negotiation, mediation, and diplomacy.
Michelangelo	The Michelangelo virus is a computer virus first discovered in April 1991 in New Zealand. The virus was designed to infect DOS systems (but did not engage the operating system or make any OS calls; Michelangelo, like all boot sector viruses, basically operated at the BIOS level) and remained dormant until March 6, the birthday of Renaissance artist Michelangelo. There is no reference to the artist in the virus, and it is doubtful that the virus writer intended Michelangelo to be referenced to the virus.
Resolution	A resolution is a written motion adopted by a deliberative body. The substance of the resolution can be anything that can normally be proposed as a motion. For long or important motions, though, it is often better to have them written out so that discussion is easier or so that it can be distributed outside of the body after its adoption.
Attitude	An attitude is a hypothetical construct that represents an individual's degree of like or dislike for something. Attitudes are generally positive or negative views of a person, place, thing, or event-- this is often referred to as the attitude object. People can also be conflicted or ambivalent toward an object, meaning that they simultaneously possess both positive and negative attitudes toward the item in question.
Cognitive complexity	Cognitive complexity describes cognition along a simplicity-complexity axis. It is the subject of academic study in fields including personal construct psychology, organisational theory and human-computer interaction. History First proposed by James Bieri in 1955.
Motivation	Motivation is the driving force which help causes us to achieve goals. Motivation is said to be intrinsic or extrinsic. The term is generally used for humans but, theoretically, it can also be used to describe the causes for animal behavior as well.

Chapter 2. Culture and Communication

Skill	A skill is the learned capacity to carry out pre-determined results often with the minimum outlay of time, energy, or both. Skills can often be divided into domain-general and domain-specific skills. For example, in the domain of work, some general skills would include time management, teamwork and leadership, self motivation and others, whereas domain-specific skills would be useful only for a certain job.
Ambiguity	Ambiguity, in law, is of two kinds, patent and latent.
	Patent ambiguity is that ambiguity which is apparent on the face of an instrument to any one perusing it, even if he be unacquainted with the circumstances of the parties. In the case of a patent ambiguity parol evidence is admissible to explain only what has been written, not what it was intended to write.
Ethnocentrism	Ethnocentrism is the tendency to believe that one's ethnic or cultural group is centrally important, and that all other groups are measured in relation to one's own. The ethnocentric individual will judge other groups relative to his or her own particular ethnic group or culture, especially with concern to language, behavior, customs, and religion. These ethnic distinctions and sub-divisions serve to define each ethnicity's unique cultural identity.
Collaboration	Collaboration is a recursive process where two or more people or organizations work together to realize shared goals, -- for example, an intruiging endeavor that is creative in nature--by sharing knowledge, learning and building consensus. Most collaboration requires leadership, although the form of leadership can be social within a decentralized and egalitarian group. In particular, teams that work collaboratively can obtain greater resources, recognition and reward when facing competition for finite resources.
Prejudice	A prejudice is a prejudgment, an assumption made about someone or something before having adequate knowledge to be able to do so with guaranteed accuracy. The word prejudice is most commonly used to refer to a preconceived judgment toward a people or a person because of race, social class, gender, ethnicity, homelessness, age, disability, obesity, religion, sexual orientation or other personal characteristics. It also means beliefs without knowledge of the facts and may include 'any unreasonable attitude that is unusually resistant to rational influence.' Common misconceptions

At times, the terms prejudice and stereotype might be confusing:

- Prejudices are abstract-general preconceptions or abstract-general attitudes towards any type of situations, object, or person.
- Stereotypes are generalizations of existing characteristics that reduce complexity.

.

Speech

Speech is the vocalized form of human communication. It is based upon the syntactic combination of lexicals and names that are drawn from very large (usually >10,000 different words) vocabularies. Each spoken word is created out of the phonetic combination of a limited set of vowel and consonant speech sound units.

Issue

In law, issue can mean several things:

- In wills and trusts, a person's issue are his or her lineal descendants or offspring. These are distinguished from heirs, which can include other kin such as a brother, sister, mother, father, grandfather, uncle, aunt, nephew, niece, or cousin.

- In corporations and business associations law, issue can refer to areas involving stocks.

- In evidence as well as civil and criminal procedure, there are issues of fact. Issues of fact are rhetorically presented by statements of fact which are each put to a test: Is the statement true or false?

Often, different parties have conflicting statements of fact.

Mindfulness

Modern clinical psychology and psychiatry since the 1970s have developed a number of therapeutic applications based on the concept of mindfulness in Buddhist meditation.

Definitions

Several definitions of mindfulness have been used in modern Western psychology. According to various prominent psychological definitions, Mindfulness refers to a psychological quality that involves

bringing one's complete attention to the present experience on a moment-to-moment basis,

or involves

paying attention in a particular way: on purpose, in the present moment, and nonjudgmentally,

or involves

a kind of nonelaborative, nonjudgmental, present-centered awareness in which each thought, feeling, or sensation that arises in the attentional field is acknowledged and accepted as it is

Bishop, Lau, and colleagues (2007) offered a two component model of mindfulness:

The first component [of mindfulness] involves the self-regulation of attention so that it is maintained on immediate experience, thereby allowing for increased recognition of mental events in the present moment.

Conflict resolution	Conflict resolution is a range of methods of eliminating sources of conflict. The term 'conflict resolution' is sometimes used interchangeably with the term dispute resolution or alternative dispute resolution. Processes of conflict resolution generally include negotiation, mediation, and diplomacy.
Resolution	A resolution is a written motion adopted by a deliberative body. The substance of the resolution can be anything that can normally be proposed as a motion. For long or important motions, though, it is often better to have them written out so that discussion is easier or so that it can be distributed outside of the body after its adoption.
Self-esteem	Self-esteem is a term used in psychology to reflect a person's overall evaluation or appraisal of his or her own worth. Self-esteem encompasses beliefs (for example, 'I am competent', 'I am worthy') and emotions such as triumph, despair, pride and shame. Self-esteem can apply specifically to a particular dimension (for example, 'I believe I am a good writer and I feel happy about that') or have global extent (for example, 'I believe I am a bad person, and feel bad of myself in general').
Erikson's stages of psychosocial development	Erikson's stages of psychosocial development as articulated by Erik Erikson explain eight stages through which a healthily developing human should pass from infancy to late adulthood. In each stage the person confronts, and hopefully masters, new challenges. Each stage builds on the successful completion of earlier stages.
Michelangelo	The Michelangelo virus is a computer virus first discovered in April 1991 in New Zealand. The virus was designed to infect DOS systems (but did not engage the operating system or make any OS calls; Michelangelo, like all boot sector viruses, basically operated at the BIOS level) and remained dormant until March 6, the birthday of Renaissance artist Michelangelo. There is no reference to the artist in the virus, and it is doubtful that the virus writer intended Michelangelo to be referenced to the virus.
Group	In the social sciences a group can be defined as two or more humans who interact with one another, accept expectations and obligations as members of the group, and share a common identity. By this definition, society can be viewed as a large group, though most social groups are considerably smaller. A true group exhibits some degree of social cohesion and is more than a simple collection or aggregate of individuals, such as people waiting at a bus stop.

Chapter 3. Communication and the Self

Reference group	A reference group is a concept referring to a group to which an individual or another group is compared. Sociologists call any group that individuals use as a standard for evaluating themselves and their own behavior a reference group. Reference groups are used in order to evaluate and determine the nature of a given individual or other group's characteristics and sociological attributes.
Space	Space is the boundless, three-dimensional extent in which objects and events occur and have relative position and direction. Physical space is often conceived in three linear dimensions, although modern physicists usually consider it, with time, to be part of the boundless four-dimensional continuum known as spacetime. In mathematics one examines 'spaces' with different numbers of dimensions and with different underlying structures.
Variation	In sociolinguistics, variation in language use among speakers or groups of speakers is a principal concern. Such variation may occur in pronunciation (accent), word choice (lexicon), or even preferences for particular grammatical patterns. Studies of language variation and its correlation with sociological categories, such as William Labov's 1963 paper 'The social motivation of a sound change,' led to the foundation of sociolinguistics as a sub-field of linguistics.
Resistance	'Resistance' as initially used by Sigmund Freud, referred to patients blocking memories from conscious memory. This was a key concept, since the primary treatment method of Freud's talk therapy required making these memories available to the patient's consciousness. 'Resistance' expanded Later, Freud described five different forms of resistance.

Chapter 3. Communication and the Self

Publics	Publics are small groups of people who follow one or more particular issue very closely. They are well informed about the issue(s) and also have a very strong opinion on it/them. They tend to know more about politics than the average person, and, therefore, exert more influence, because these people care so deeply about their cause(s) that they donate much time and money.
Identity	Identity is an umbrella term used throughout the social sciences to describe a person's conception and expression of their individuality or group affiliations (such as national identity and cultural identity). The term is used more specifically in psychology and sociology, including the two forms of social psychology. The term is also used with respect to place identity.
Collaboration	Collaboration is a recursive process where two or more people or organizations work together to realize shared goals, -- for example, an intruiging endeavor that is creative in nature--by sharing knowledge, learning and building consensus. Most collaboration requires leadership, although the form of leadership can be social within a decentralized and egalitarian group. In particular, teams that work collaboratively can obtain greater resources, recognition and reward when facing competition for finite resources.
Favor	As an activity, a favor is voluntarily provided. It may be defined as something done or granted out of goodwill, rather than from justice or payment. Yet, reciprocity (responding to a positive action with another positive action) may be a common motivation, but other motivations, e.g. altruism may rather be the main ones where the action isn't to return the favor but to pay it forward.
Clothing	Clothing refers to any covering for the human body. The wearing of clothing is exclusively a human characteristic and is a feature of most human societies. The amount and type of clothing worn depends on functional considerations (such as a need for warmth or protection from the elements) and social considerations.
Interaction	In statistics, an interaction may arise when considering the relationship among three or more variables, and describes a situation in which the simultaneous influence of two variables on a third is not additive. Most commonly, interactions are considered in the context of regression analyses.

Clam101

	The presence of interactions can have important implications for the interpretation of statistical models.
Manners	In sociology, manners are the unenforced standards of conduct which demonstrate that a person is proper, polite, and refined. They are like laws in that they codify or set a standard for human behavior, but they are unlike laws in that there is no formal system for punishing transgressions, other than social disapproval. They are a kind of norm.
Computer-mediated communication	Computer-mediated communication is defined as any communicative transaction that occurs through the use of two or more networked computers. While the term has traditionally referred to those communications that occur via computer-mediated formats (e.g., instant messages, e-mails, chat rooms), it has also been applied to other forms of text-based interaction such as text messaging. Research on Computer mediated communication focuses largely on the social effects of different computer-supported communication technologies.

Chapter 4. Perceiving Others

Space	Space is the boundless, three-dimensional extent in which objects and events occur and have relative position and direction. Physical space is often conceived in three linear dimensions, although modern physicists usually consider it, with time, to be part of the boundless four-dimensional continuum known as spacetime. In mathematics one examines 'spaces' with different numbers of dimensions and with different underlying structures.
Dyad	A dyad in sociology is a noun used to describe a group of two people. 'Dyadic' is an adjective used to describe this type of communication/interaction. A dyad is the smallest possible social group.
Michelangelo	The Michelangelo virus is a computer virus first discovered in April 1991 in New Zealand. The virus was designed to infect DOS systems (but did not engage the operating system or make any OS calls; Michelangelo, like all boot sector viruses, basically operated at the BIOS level) and remained dormant until March 6, the birthday of Renaissance artist Michelangelo. There is no reference to the artist in the virus, and it is doubtful that the virus writer intended Michelangelo to be referenced to the virus.
Interaction	In statistics, an interaction may arise when considering the relationship among three or more variables, and describes a situation in which the simultaneous influence of two variables on a third is not additive. Most commonly, interactions are considered in the context of regression analyses. The presence of interactions can have important implications for the interpretation of statistical models.
Publics	Publics are small groups of people who follow one or more particular issue very closely. They are well informed about the issue(s) and also have a very strong opinion on it/them. They tend to know more about politics than the average person, and, therefore, exert more influence, because these people care so deeply about their cause(s) that they donate much time and money.

Chapter 4. Perceiving Others

Schema	A schema in psychology and cognitive science, describes any of several concepts including: • An organized pattern of thought or behavior. • A structured cluster of pre-conceived ideas. • A mental structure that represents some aspect of the world. • A specific knowledge structure or cognitive representation of the self. • A mental framework centering on a specific theme, that helps us to organize social information. • Structures that organize our knowledge and assumptions about something and are used for interpreting and processing information. A schema for oneself is called a 'self schema'. Schemata for other people are called 'person schemata'.
Computer-mediated communication	Computer-mediated communication is defined as any communicative transaction that occurs through the use of two or more networked computers. While the term has traditionally referred to those communications that occur via computer-mediated formats (e.g., instant messages, e-mails, chat rooms), it has also been applied to other forms of text-based interaction such as text messaging. Research on Computer mediated communication focuses largely on the social effects of different computer-supported communication technologies.
Interpersonal communication	Interpersonal communication is usually defined by communication scholars in numerous ways, usually describing participants who are dependent upon one another and have a shared history. It can involve one on one conversations or individuals interacting with many people within a society. It helps us understand how and why people behave and communicate in different ways to construct and negotiate a social reality.
Interpersonal relationship	An interpersonal relationship is an association between two or more people that may range from fleeting to enduring. This association may be based on limerence, love, solidarity, regular business interactions, or some other type of social commitment. Interpersonal relationships are formed in the context of social, cultural and other influences.
Narrative	A narrative is a story that is created in a constructive format (as a work of speech, writing, song, film, television, video games, photography or theatre) that describes a sequence of fictional or non-fictional events. Ultimately its origin is found in the Proto-Indo-European root gno-, 'to know'.

Chapter 4. Perceiving Others

	The word 'story' may be used as a synonym of 'narrative', but can also be used to refer to the sequence of events described in a narrative.
Negotiation	In the BDSM community, negotiation is a form of communication where participants make arrangements on each others' requirements, responsibilities, and limits to find the best possible agreement.

Activity within BDSM relationships requires trust, openness about most practices that may include risks. On the other hand, partners have certain needs which should be clearly defined in order to be properly satisfied. |
Conflict resolution	Conflict resolution is a range of methods of eliminating sources of conflict. The term 'conflict resolution' is sometimes used interchangeably with the term dispute resolution or alternative dispute resolution. Processes of conflict resolution generally include negotiation, mediation, and diplomacy.
Resolution	A resolution is a written motion adopted by a deliberative body. The substance of the resolution can be anything that can normally be proposed as a motion. For long or important motions, though, it is often better to have them written out so that discussion is easier or so that it can be distributed outside of the body after its adoption.
Homophobia	Homophobia is a range of negative attitudes and feelings towards lesbian, gay, bisexual, and in some cases transgender and intersex people and behaviour. Definitions refer variably to antipathy, contempt, prejudice, aversion, and irrational fear. Homophobia is observable in critical and hostile behavior such as discrimination and violence on the basis of a perceived non-heterosexual orientation.
Gender	Gender is a set of characteristics distinguishing between male and female, particularly in the cases of men and women. Depending on the context, the discriminating characteristics vary from sex to social role to gender identity. In 1955, sexologist John Money, introduced the terminological distinction between biological sex and gender as a role.

Clam101

Chapter 4. Perceiving Others

Gender role	Gender roles refers to the set of social and behavioral norms that are considered to be socially appropriate for individuals of a specific sex in the context of a specific culture, which differ widely between cultures and over time. There are differences of opinion as to whether observed gender differences in behavior and personality characteristics are, at least in part, due to cultural or social factors, and therefore, the product of socialization experiences, or to what extent gender differences are due to biological and physiological differences. Views on gender-based differentiation in the workplace and in interpersonal relationships have often undergone profound changes as a result of feminist and/or economic influences, but there are still considerable differences in gender roles in almost all societies.
Social influence	Social influence occurs when an individual's thoughts, feelings or actions are affected by other people. Social influence takes many forms and can be seen in conformity, socialization, peer pressure, obedience, leadership, persuasion, sales, and marketing. In 1958, Harvard psychologist, Herbert Kelman identified three broad varieties of social influence.
Standpoint theory	Standpoint theory is a postmodern method for analyzing inter-subjective discourses. 'Developed primarily by social scientists, especially sociologists ' political theorists. It extends some of the early insights about consciousness that emerged from Marxist/socialist feminist theories and the wider conversations about identity politics.
Difference	Difference is a key concept of continental philosophy, denoting the process or set of properties by which one entity is distinguished from another within a relational field or a given conceptual system. In the Western philosophical system, difference is traditionally viewed as being opposed to identity, following the Principles of Leibniz, and in particular his Law of the Identity of indiscernibles. In structuralist and poststructuralist accounts, however, difference is understood to be constitutive of both meaning and identity.
Prison	A prison is a place in which people are physically confined and, usually, deprived of a range of personal freedoms. Imprisonment or incarceration is a legal penalty that may be imposed by the state for the commission of a crime. Other terms are penitentiary, correctional facility, remand center, detention center and gaol (or jail).
Attribution	Attribution is a concept in social psychology referring to how individuals explain causes of behavior and events. Attribution theory is an umbrella term for various theories that attempt to explain these processes. Fritz Heider first proposed a theory of attribution The Psychology of Interpersonal Relations.

Chapter 4. Perceiving Others

Speed dating	Speed dating is a formalized matchmaking process or dating system whose purpose is to encourage people to meet a large number of new people. Its origins are credited to Rabbi Yaacov Deyo of Aish HaTorah, originally as a way to help Jewish singles meet and marry. 'SpeedDating', as a single word, is a registered trademark of Aish HaTorah.
Halo effect	The halo effect is a cognitive bias whereby the perception of one trait (i.e. a characteristic of a person or object) is influenced by the perception of another trait (or several traits) of that person or object. An example would be judging a good-looking person as more intelligent. Edward L. Thorndike was the first to support the halo effect with empirical research.
Self-serving bias	A self-serving bias occurs when people attribute their successes to internal or personal factors but attribute their failures to situational factors beyond their control. The self-serving bias can be seen in the common human tendency to take credit for success but to deny responsibility for failure. It may also manifest itself as a tendency for people to evaluate ambiguous information in a way that is beneficial to their interests.
Emotional contagion	Emotional contagion is the tendency to catch and feel emotions that are similar to and influenced by those of others. One view developed by John Cacioppo of the underlying mechanism is that it represents a tendency to automatically mimic and synchronize facial expressions, vocalizations, postures, and movements with those of another person and, consequently, to converge emotionally. A broader definition of the phenomenon was suggested by Sigal G. Barsade--'a process in which a person or group influences the emotions or behavior of another person or group through the conscious or unconscious induction of emotion states and behavioral attitudes'.
Perspective	Perspective in pharmacoeconomics refers to the economic vantage point that is being taken in a pharmacoeconomic analysis, such as a cost-effectiveness analysis or cost-utility analysis. This will affect the types of costs (resource expenditures) and benefits that will be considered relevant to the analysis. Five general perspectives that are often cited in pharmacoeconomics include: institutional, third party, patient, governmental and societal.

CtamIOI

Chapter 4. Perceiving Others

Self-esteem	Self-esteem is a term used in psychology to reflect a person's overall evaluation or appraisal of his or her own worth. Self-esteem encompasses beliefs (for example, 'I am competent', 'I am worthy') and emotions such as triumph, despair, pride and shame. Self-esteem can apply specifically to a particular dimension (for example, 'I believe I am a good writer and I feel happy about that') or have global extent (for example, 'I believe I am a bad person, and feel bad of myself in general').
Compassion	Compassion is a virtue --one in which the emotional capacities of empathy and sympathy (for the suffering of others) are regarded as a part of love itself, and a cornerstone of greater social interconnectedness and humanism --foundational to the highest principles in philosophy, society, and personhood.
	There is an aspect of compassion which regards a quantitative dimension, such that individual's compassion is often given a property of 'depth,' 'vigour,' or 'passion.' More vigorous than empathy, the feeling commonly gives rise to an active desire to alleviate another's suffering. It is often, though not inevitably, the key component in what manifests in the social context as altruism.
Compassion fatigue	Compassion fatigue is a condition characterised by a gradual lessening of compassion over time. It is common among trauma victims and individuals that work directly with trauma victims. It was first diagnosed in nurses in the 1950s.
Empathy	Empathy is the capacity to recognize and, to some extent, share feelings (such as sadness or happiness) that are being experienced by another semi-sentient being. Someone may need to have a certain amount of empathy before they are able to feel compassion.
	Etymology
	The English word is derived from the Greek word ?μπ?θεια (empatheia), 'physical affection, passion, partiality' which comes from ?v (en), 'in, at' + π?θος (pathos), 'passion' or 'suffering'.
Ethics	Ethics, is a branch of philosophy that addresses questions about morality--that is, concepts such as good and evil, right and wrong, virtue and vice, justice, etc.

Major branches of ethics include:

- Meta-ethics, about the theoretical meaning and reference of moral propositions and how their truth-values (if any) may be determined;
- Normative ethics, about the practical means of determining a moral course of action;
- Applied ethics, about how moral outcomes can be achieved in specific situations;
- Moral psychology, about how moral capacity or moral agency develops and what its nature is;
- Descriptive ethics, about what moral values people actually abide by.

Within each of these branches are many different schools of thought and still further sub-fields of study.

Meta-ethics

Meta-ethics is the branch of ethics that seeks to understand the nature of ethical properties, and ethical statements, attitudes, and judgments.

Language

Language may refer either to the specifically human capacity for acquiring and using complex systems of communication, or to a specific instance of such a system of complex communication. The scientific study of language in any of its senses is called linguistics.

The approximately 3000-6000 languages that are spoken by humans today are the most salient examples, but natural languages can also be based on visual rather than auditive stimuli, for example in sign languages and written language.

Trust

A special trust is a business entity formed with intent to monopolize business, to restrain trade, or to fix prices. Trusts gained economic power in the U.S. in the late 19th and early 20th centuries. Some, but not all, were organized as trusts in the legal sense.

Chapter 4. Perceiving Others

Friendship	Friendship is a form of interpersonal relationship generally considered to be closer than association, although there is a range of degrees of intimacy in both friendships and associations. Friendship and association can be thought of as spanning across the same continuum. The study of friendship is included in the fields of sociology, social psychology, anthropology, philosophy, and zoology.

Chapter 5. Language

Language	Language may refer either to the specifically human capacity for acquiring and using complex systems of communication, or to a specific instance of such a system of complex communication. The scientific study of language in any of its senses is called linguistics. The approximately 3000-6000 languages that are spoken by humans today are the most salient examples, but natural languages can also be based on visual rather than auditive stimuli, for example in sign languages and written language.
Sign language	A sign language is a language which, instead of acoustically conveyed sound patterns, uses visually transmitted sign patterns (manual communication, body language) to convey meaning-- simultaneously combining hand shapes, orientation and movement of the hands, arms or body, and facial expressions to fluidly express a speaker's thoughts. Wherever communities of deaf people exist, sign languages develop. Their complex spatial grammars are markedly different from the grammars of spoken languages.
Conflict resolution	Conflict resolution is a range of methods of eliminating sources of conflict. The term 'conflict resolution' is sometimes used interchangeably with the term dispute resolution or alternative dispute resolution. Processes of conflict resolution generally include negotiation, mediation, and diplomacy.
Resolution	A resolution is a written motion adopted by a deliberative body. The substance of the resolution can be anything that can normally be proposed as a motion. For long or important motions, though, it is often better to have them written out so that discussion is easier or so that it can be distributed outside of the body after its adoption.
Space	Space is the boundless, three-dimensional extent in which objects and events occur and have relative position and direction. Physical space is often conceived in three linear dimensions, although modern physicists usually consider it, with time, to be part of the boundless four-dimensional continuum known as spacetime. In mathematics one examines 'spaces' with different numbers of dimensions and with different underlying structures.

Chapter 5. Language

Dialect	The term dialect is used in two distinct ways, even by linguists. One usage refers to a variety of a language that is a characteristic of a particular group of the language's speakers. The term is applied most often to regional speech patterns, but a dialect may also be defined by other factors, such as social class.
Coordinated Management of Meaning	Coordinated Management of Meaning is a practical theory that sees communication as doing things fully as much as talking about them. 'Taking the communication perspective' consists of looking at communication (rather than through it to what it is ostensibly about) and seeing it as a two-sided process of (1) coordinating actions with others, and (2) making/managing meanings. These interwoven threads of stories and actions comprise the texture of social worlds.
Linguistics	Linguistics is the scientific study of human language. Linguistics can be broadly broken into three categories or subfields: the study of language form, of language meaning, and of language in context.
	The first is the study of language structure, or grammar.
Relativism	Relativism is the concept that points of view have no absolute truth or validity, having only relative, subjective value according to differences in perception and consideration. The term is often used to refer to the context of moral principle, where in a relativistic mode of thought, principles and ethics are regarded as applicable in only limited context. There are many forms of relativism which vary in their degree of controversy.
Identity	Identity is an umbrella term used throughout the social sciences to describe a person's conception and expression of their individuality or group affiliations (such as national identity and cultural identity). The term is used more specifically in psychology and sociology, including the two forms of social psychology. The term is also used with respect to place identity.
Lagniappe	A lagniappe is a small gift given to a customer by a merchant at the time of a purchase (such as a 13th donut when buying a dozen), or more broadly, 'something given or obtained gratuitously or by way of good measure.' The word is chiefly used in the Gulf Coast of the United States, especially Louisiana.

Chapter 5. Language

The word entered English from Louisiana French, in turn derived from the American Spanish phrase la ñapa ('something that is added'). The term has been traced back to the Quechua word yapay ('to increase; to add').

Family	In human context, a family is a group of people affiliated by consanguinity, affinity, or co-residence. In most societies it is the principal institution for the socialization of children. Extended from the human 'family unit' by biological-cultural affinity, marriage, economy, culture, tradition, honor, and friendship are concepts of family that are physical and metaphorical, or that grow increasingly inclusive extending to community, village, city, region, nationhood, global village and humanism.
Affiliation	In law, affiliation is the term to describe a partnership between two or more parties.

Affiliation procedures in England

In England a number of statutes on the subject have been passed, the chief being the Bastardy Act of the Parliament of 1845, and the Bastardy Laws Amendment Acts of 1872 and 1873. The mother of a bastard may summon the putative father to petty sessions within 12 months of the birth (or at any later time if he is proved to have contributed to the child's support within 12 months after the birth), and the justices, as after hearing evidence on both sides, may, if the mother's evidence be corroborated in some material particular, adjudge the man to be the putative father] of the child, and order him to pay a sum not exceeding five shillings a week for its maintenance, together with a sum for expenses incidental to the birth, or the funeral expenses, if it has died before the date of order, and the costs of the proceedings.

ceases to be valid after the child reaches the age of 13, but the justices (also referred to as Gold writers under these circumstances) may in the order direct the payments to be continued until the child is 16 years of age. |
| Credibility | Credibility refers to the objective and subjective components of the believability of a source or message. |

Traditionally, credibility has two key components: trustworthiness and expertise, which both have objective and subjective components. Trustworthiness is based more on subjective factors, but can include objective measurements such as established reliability.

Interest

Interest is a fee paid on borrowed assets. It is the price paid for the use of borrowed money, or, money earned by deposited funds. Assets that are sometimes lent with interest include money, shares, consumer goods through hire purchase, major assets such as aircraft, and even entire factories in finance lease arrangements.

Vocabulary

A person's vocabulary is the set of words within a language that are familiar to that person. A vocabulary usually grows and evolves with age, and serves as a useful and fundamental tool for communication and acquiring knowledge. Acquiring an extensive vocabulary is one of the largest challenges in learning a second language.

Convergence

Convergence in sustainability sciences refers to mechanisms and pathways that lead towards sustainability with a specific focus on 'Equity within biological planetary limits'. These pathways and mechanisms explicitly advocate equity and recognise the need for redistribution of the Earth's resources in order for human society to operate enduringly within the Earth's biophysical limits.

This use of the term 'convergence' harks from the concept of contraction and convergence taking its core principles of Equity and Survival and applying them beyond the frame of greenhouse gas emissions to the wider sustainability agenda.

Power

In physics, power is the rate at which work is performed or energy is converted As a simple example, if an elevated reservoir is used to drive a waterwheel, then replacing its drain valve with another of larger diameter does not change the water's potential energy, but does increase the available power because the larger valve allows higher flow, so the potential energy can be more quickly converted into kinetic energy.

Chapter 5. Language

If ΔW is the amount of work performed during a period of time of duration Δt, the average power P_{avg} over that period is given by the formula

$$P_{avg} = \frac{\Delta W}{\Delta t} \, .$$

It is the average amount of work done or energy converted per unit of time. The average power is often simply called 'power' when the context makes it clear.

Speech

Speech is the vocalized form of human communication. It is based upon the syntactic combination of lexicals and names that are drawn from very large (usually >10,000 different words) vocabularies. Each spoken word is created out of the phonetic combination of a limited set of vowel and consonant speech sound units.

Gender

Gender is a set of characteristics distinguishing between male and female, particularly in the cases of men and women. Depending on the context, the discriminating characteristics vary from sex to social role to gender identity. In 1955, sexologist John Money, introduced the terminological distinction between biological sex and gender as a role.

Abuse

Abuse is the improper usage or treatment for a bad purpose, often to unfairly or improperly gain benefit, physical or verbal maltreatment, injury, sexual assault, violation, rape, unjust practices; wrongful practice or custom; offense; crime, or otherwise verbal aggression. Abuse can come in many forms.

Abuses such as verbal abuse and physical abuse can be consensual within the confines of erotic humiliation and BDSM.

Satanic ritual abuse was simply a moral panic and not substantiated as a credible type of abuse.

Chapter 5. Language

Precision	In statistics, the term precision can mean a quantity defined in a specific way. This is in addition to its more general meaning in the contexts of accuracy and precision and of precision and recall. There can be differences in usage of the term for particular statistical models but, in general statistical usage, the precision is defined to be the reciprocal of the variance, while the precision matrix is the matrix inverse of the covariance matrix.
Ambiguity	Ambiguity, in law, is of two kinds, patent and latent. Patent ambiguity is that ambiguity which is apparent on the face of an instrument to any one perusing it, even if he be unacquainted with the circumstances of the parties. In the case of a patent ambiguity parol evidence is admissible to explain only what has been written, not what it was intended to write.
Abstraction	Abstraction is the process or result of generalization by reducing the information content of a concept or an observable phenomenon, typically to retain only information which is relevant for a particular purpose. For example, abstracting a leather soccer ball to a ball retains only the information on general ball attributes and behaviour. Similarly, abstracting happiness to an emotional state reduces the amount of information conveyed about the emotional state.
College	A college is an educational institution or a constituent part of an educational institution. Usage varies in English-speaking nations. A college may be a degree-awarding tertiary educational institution, an institution within a federal university, an institution offering vocational education, or a secondary school.
Euphemism	Euphemism is a substitution for an expression that may offend or suggest something unpleasant to the receiver, using instead an agreeable or less offensive expression, or to make it less troublesome for the speaker.

Chapter 5. Language

	Some euphemisms are intended to amuse, while others are created to mislead. Usage When a phrase is used as a euphemism, it often becomes a metaphor whose literal meaning is dropped.
Narcissism	Narcissism is the personality trait of egotism, vanity, conceit, or simple selfishness. Applied to a social group, it is sometimes used to denote elitism or an indifference to the plight of others. The name 'narcissism' was coined by Freud after Narcissus who in Greek myth was a pathologically self-absorbed young man who fell in love with his own reflection in a pool.
Emotive	'Emotional expressions', also called 'emotives' are an effort by the speaker to offer an interpretation of something that is observable to no other actor (Reddy 1997). If emotions are feelings, emotives are the expressions of those feelings through the use of language, specifically through constructions that explicitly describe emotional states or attitudes. (Luke 2004).
Computer-mediated communication	Computer-mediated communication is defined as any communicative transaction that occurs through the use of two or more networked computers. While the term has traditionally referred to those communications that occur via computer-mediated formats (e.g., instant messages, e-mails, chat rooms), it has also been applied to other forms of text-based interaction such as text messaging. Research on Computer mediated communication focuses largely on the social effects of different computer-supported communication technologies.
Homosexuality	Homosexuality is romantic and/or sexual attraction or behavior among members of the same sex or gender. As a sexual orientation, homosexuality refers to 'an enduring pattern of or disposition to experience sexual, affectional, or romantic attractions' primarily or exclusively to people of the same sex; 'it also refers to an individual's sense of personal and social identity based on those attractions, behaviors expressing them, and membership in a community of others who share them.'

Chapter 5. Language

Homosexuality is one of the three main categories of sexual orientation, along with bisexuality and heterosexuality, within the heterosexual-homosexual continuum. The consensus of the behavioral and social sciences and the health and mental health professions is that homosexuality is a normal and positive variation in human sexual orientation, though many religious societies, including Catholicism, Mormonism, and Islam, and some psychological associations, such as NARTH, have traditionally taught that homosexual activity is sinful or dysfunctional.

Sexual orientation

Sexual orientation describes a pattern of emotional, romantic, or sexual attraction to the opposite gender, same gender, both genders, neither gender, or another gender. According to the American Psychological Association, sexual orientation is enduring and also refers to a person's sense of 'personal and social identity based on those attractions, behaviors expressing them, and membership in a community of others who share them.' The current consensus among scholars is that sexual orientation is not a choice. No simple, single cause for sexual orientation has been conclusively demonstrated, but research suggests that it is by a combination of genetic, hormonal, and environmental influences, with biological factors involving a complex interplay of genetic factors and the early uterine environment.

Chapter 6. Nonverbal Communication

Nonverbal communication	Nonverbal communication is usually understood as the process of communication through sending and receiving wordless messages. i.e., language is not the only source of communication, there are other means also. Messages can be communicated through gestures and touch (Haptic communication), by body language or posture, by facial expression and eye contact.
Family	In human context, a family is a group of people affiliated by consanguinity, affinity, or co-residence. In most societies it is the principal institution for the socialization of children. Extended from the human 'family unit' by biological-cultural affinity, marriage, economy, culture, tradition, honor, and friendship are concepts of family that are physical and metaphorical, or that grow increasingly inclusive extending to community, village, city, region, nationhood, global village and humanism.
Ambiguity	Ambiguity, in law, is of two kinds, patent and latent. Patent ambiguity is that ambiguity which is apparent on the face of an instrument to any one perusing it, even if he be unacquainted with the circumstances of the parties. In the case of a patent ambiguity parol evidence is admissible to explain only what has been written, not what it was intended to write.
Prince	Prince is a general term for a ruler, monarch or member of a monarch's or former monarch's family, and is a hereditary title in the nobility of some European states. The feminine equivalent is a princess. The English word derives, via the French word prince, from the Latin noun princeps, from primus(first) + capio(to seize), meaning 'the chief, most distinguished, ruler, prince'.
Contact	In family law, contact is one of the general terms which denotes the level of contact a parent or other significant person in a child's life can have with that child. Contact forms part of the bundle of rights and privileges which a parent may have in relation to any child of the family. Following ratification of the United Nations Convention on the Rights of the Child in most countries, the term 'access' was superseded by the term contact.

Clam101

Chapter 6. Nonverbal Communication

Eye contact	Eye contact is a meeting of the eyes between two individuals. In human beings, eye contact is a form of nonverbal communication and is thought to have a large influence on social behavior. Coined in the early to mid-1960s, the term has come in the West to often define the act as a meaningful and important sign of confidence and social communication.
Interaction	In statistics, an interaction may arise when considering the relationship among three or more variables, and describes a situation in which the simultaneous influence of two variables on a third is not additive. Most commonly, interactions are considered in the context of regression analyses. The presence of interactions can have important implications for the interpretation of statistical models.
Lie detection	Lie detection is the practice of determining whether someone is lying. Activities of the body not easily controlled by the conscious mind are compared under different circumstances. Usually this involves asking the subject control questions where the answers are known to the examiner and comparing them to questions where the answers are not known.
Conflict resolution	Conflict resolution is a range of methods of eliminating sources of conflict. The term 'conflict resolution' is sometimes used interchangeably with the term dispute resolution or alternative dispute resolution. Processes of conflict resolution generally include negotiation, mediation, and diplomacy.
Resolution	A resolution is a written motion adopted by a deliberative body. The substance of the resolution can be anything that can normally be proposed as a motion. For long or important motions, though, it is often better to have them written out so that discussion is easier or so that it can be distributed outside of the body after its adoption.
Identity	Identity is an umbrella term used throughout the social sciences to describe a person's conception and expression of their individuality or group affiliations (such as national identity and cultural identity). The term is used more specifically in psychology and sociology, including the two forms of social psychology. The term is also used with respect to place identity.

Chapter 6. Nonverbal Communication

Manners	In sociology, manners are the unenforced standards of conduct which demonstrate that a person is proper, polite, and refined. They are like laws in that they codify or set a standard for human behavior, but they are unlike laws in that there is no formal system for punishing transgressions, other than social disapproval. They are a kind of norm.
Genie	Genie is the pseudonym for a feral child who spent nearly all of the first thirteen years of her life locked inside a bedroom strapped to a potty chair. She was a victim of one of the most severe cases of social isolation in American history. Genie was discovered by Los Angeles authorities on November 4, 1970.
Space	Space is the boundless, three-dimensional extent in which objects and events occur and have relative position and direction. Physical space is often conceived in three linear dimensions, although modern physicists usually consider it, with time, to be part of the boundless four-dimensional continuum known as spacetime. In mathematics one examines 'spaces' with different numbers of dimensions and with different underlying structures.
Kinesics	Kinesics is the interpretation of body language such as facial expressions and gestures -- or, more formally, non-verbal behavior related to movement, either of any part of the body or the body as a whole. The term was first used (in 1952) by Ray Birdwhistell, an anthropologist who wished to study how people communicate through posture, gesture, stance, and movement. Part of Birdwhistell's work involved making film of people in social situations and analyzing them to show different levels of communication not clearly seen otherwise.
Posture	Primarily, posture is a reflex to keep the body upright.
Michelangelo	The Michelangelo virus is a computer virus first discovered in April 1991 in New Zealand. The virus was designed to infect DOS systems (but did not engage the operating system or make any OS calls; Michelangelo, like all boot sector viruses, basically operated at the BIOS level) and remained dormant until March 6, the birthday of Renaissance artist Michelangelo. There is no reference to the artist in the virus, and it is doubtful that the virus writer intended Michelangelo to be referenced to the virus.

Chapter 6. Nonverbal Communication

Mirroring	Mirroring is the behaviour in which one person copies another person usually while in social interaction with them. It may include miming gestures, movements, body language, muscle tensions, expressions, tones, eye movements, breathing, tempo, accent, attitude, choice of words/metaphors and other aspects of communication. It is often observed among couples or close friends.
Paralanguage	Paralanguage refers to the non-verbal elements of communication used to modify meaning and convey emotion. Paralanguage may be expressed consciously or unconsciously, and it includes the pitch, volume, and, in some cases, intonation of speech. Sometimes the definition is restricted to vocally-produced sounds.
Sarcasm	Sarcasm is 'a sharp, bitter, or cutting expression or remark; a bitter jibe or taunt.' Though irony is usually the immediate context, most authorities sharply distinguish sarcasm from irony; however, others argue that sarcasm may or often does involve irony or employs ambivalence. Sarcasm has been suggested as a possible bullying action in some circumstances. Origin of the term It is first recorded in English in 1579, in an annotation to The Shepheardes Calender: October: The word comes from the late Greek σαρκαζμ?ς (sarkazmos) taken from the word σαρκ?ζειν meaning 'to tear flesh, gnash the teeth, speak bitterly'.
Personal space	Personal space is the region surrounding a person which they regard as psychologically theirs. Invasion of personal space often leads to discomfort, anger, or anxiety on the part of the victim. The notion of personal space comes from Edward T. Hall, whose ideas were influenced by Heini Hediger's studies of behavior of zoo animals.
Proxemics	The term proxemics was introduced by anthropologist Edward T. Hall in 1966. Proxemics is the study of set measurable distances between people as they interact. The effects of proxemics, according to Hall, can be summarized by the following loose rule:

In animals, German zoologist Heini Heidger had distinguished between flight distance (run boundary), critical distance (attack boundary), personal distance (distance separating members of non-contact species, as a pair of swans), and social distance (intraspecies communication distance). Hall reasoned that, with very few exceptions, flight distance and critical distance have been eliminated in human reactions, and thus interviewed hundreds of people to determine modified criteria for human interactions.

Homosexuality	Homosexuality is romantic and/or sexual attraction or behavior among members of the same sex or gender. As a sexual orientation, homosexuality refers to 'an enduring pattern of or disposition to experience sexual, affectional, or romantic attractions' primarily or exclusively to people of the same sex; 'it also refers to an individual's sense of personal and social identity based on those attractions, behaviors expressing them, and membership in a community of others who share them.' Homosexuality is one of the three main categories of sexual orientation, along with bisexuality and heterosexuality, within the heterosexual-homosexual continuum. The consensus of the behavioral and social sciences and the health and mental health professions is that homosexuality is a normal and positive variation in human sexual orientation, though many religious societies, including Catholicism, Mormonism, and Islam, and some psychological associations, such as NARTH, have traditionally taught that homosexual activity is sinful or dysfunctional.
Obstacle	An obstacle, is an object, thing, action or situation that causes an obstruction, forms a barrier, creates a difficulty, a nuisance or a disorder to achieve concrete goals. There are, therefore, different types of obstacles, which can be physical, economic, biopsychosocial, cultural, political, technological or even military. Physical barriers As physical obstacles, we can enumerate all those physical barriers that block the action and prevent the progress or the achievement of a concrete goal.

Chapter 6. Nonverbal Communication

Publics	Publics are small groups of people who follow one or more particular issue very closely. They are well informed about the issue(s) and also have a very strong opinion on it/them. They tend to know more about politics than the average person, and, therefore, exert more influence, because these people care so deeply about their cause(s) that they donate much time and money.
Social distance	Social distance describes the distance between different groups of society and is opposed to locational distance. The notion includes all differences such as social class, race/ethnicity or sexuality, but also the fact that the different groups do not mix. The term is often applied in cities, but its use is not limited to that.
Territoriality	Territoriality is a term associated with nonverbal communication that refers to how people use space to communicate ownership/occupancy of areas and possessions (Beebe, Beebe ' Redmond 2008, p. 209). The anthropological concept branches from the observations of animal ownership behaviors. We can consider that this personal space is like a bubble that one doesn't want invaded.
Chronemics	Chronemics is the study of the use of time in nonverbal communication. The way we perceive time, structure our time and react to time is a powerful communication tool, and helps set the stage for the communication process. Across cultures, time perception plays a large role in the nonverbal communication process.
Clothing	Clothing refers to any covering for the human body. The wearing of clothing is exclusively a human characteristic and is a feature of most human societies. The amount and type of clothing worn depends on functional considerations (such as a need for warmth or protection from the elements) and social considerations.
Environment	The biophysical environment is the symbiosis between the physical environment and the biological life forms within the environment, and includes all variables that comprise the Earth's biosphere. The biophysical environment can be divided into two categories: the natural environment and the built environment, with some overlap between the two. Following the industrial revolution, the built environment has become an increasingly significant part of the Earth's environment.

Chapter 7. Listening, Understanding and Supporting Others

Talking circle	A talking circle, is a method used by a group to discuss a topic in an egalitarian and non-confrontational manner. The group members sit in a circle and comment on the topic of discussion following a small number of rules: 1. Only the person holding a specific object -- such as a talking stick -- may speak. 2. An effort is made to listen as you would want to be listened to when you are speaking. 3. The talking stick passes around the circle. Ideally everybody forms a seated circle shoulder-to-shoulder, so that they can see each other's faces, including those on either side of them. This becomes impractical for large circles and folks may be nested 3 or more deep so that everyone is close enough to hear.
Michelangelo	The Michelangelo virus is a computer virus first discovered in April 1991 in New Zealand. The virus was designed to infect DOS systems (but did not engage the operating system or make any OS calls; Michelangelo, like all boot sector viruses, basically operated at the BIOS level) and remained dormant until March 6, the birthday of Renaissance artist Michelangelo. There is no reference to the artist in the virus, and it is doubtful that the virus writer intended Michelangelo to be referenced to the virus.
Attitude	An attitude is a hypothetical construct that represents an individual's degree of like or dislike for something. Attitudes are generally positive or negative views of a person, place, thing, or event-- this is often referred to as the attitude object. People can also be conflicted or ambivalent toward an object, meaning that they simultaneously possess both positive and negative attitudes toward the item in question.
Impartiality	Impartiality is a principle of justice holding that decisions should be based on objective criteria, rather than on the basis of bias, prejudice, or preferring the benefit to one person over another for improper reasons. Philosophical concepts of impartiality According to Bernard Gert, 'A is impartial in respect R with regard to group G if and only if A's actions in respect R are not influenced at all by which member(s) of G benefit or are harmed by these actions.' (Gert 1995, p.104).

	Impartiality does not require, however, that individuals be treated equally under all circumstances.
Language	Language may refer either to the specifically human capacity for acquiring and using complex systems of communication, or to a specific instance of such a system of complex communication. The scientific study of language in any of its senses is called linguistics.
	The approximately 3000-6000 languages that are spoken by humans today are the most salient examples, but natural languages can also be based on visual rather than auditive stimuli, for example in sign languages and written language.
Obstacle	An obstacle, is an object, thing, action or situation that causes an obstruction, forms a barrier, creates a difficulty, a nuisance or a disorder to achieve concrete goals. There are, therefore, different types of obstacles, which can be physical, economic, biopsychosocial, cultural, political, technological or even military.
	Physical barriers
	As physical obstacles, we can enumerate all those physical barriers that block the action and prevent the progress or the achievement of a concrete goal.
Space	Space is the boundless, three-dimensional extent in which objects and events occur and have relative position and direction. Physical space is often conceived in three linear dimensions, although modern physicists usually consider it, with time, to be part of the boundless four-dimensional continuum known as spacetime. In mathematics one examines 'spaces' with different numbers of dimensions and with different underlying structures.
Counterfeit	A counterfeit is an imitation, usually one that is made with the intent of fraudulently passing it off as genuine. Counterfeit products are often produced with the intent to take advantage of the superior value of the imitated product. The word counterfeit frequently describes both the forgeries of currency and documents, as well as the imitations of works of art, clothing, software, pharmaceuticals, watches, electronics and company logos and brands.

Chapter 7. Listening, Understanding and Supporting Others

Habit	Habits are routines of behavior that are repeated regularly and tend to occur subconsciously. Habitual behavior often goes unnoticed in persons exhibiting it, because a person does not need to engage in self-analysis when undertaking routine tasks. Habituation is an extremely simple form of learning, in which an organism, after a period of exposure to a stimulus, stops responding to that stimulus in varied manners.
Narcissism	Narcissism is the personality trait of egotism, vanity, conceit, or simple selfishness. Applied to a social group, it is sometimes used to denote elitism or an indifference to the plight of others. The name 'narcissism' was coined by Freud after Narcissus who in Greek myth was a pathologically self-absorbed young man who fell in love with his own reflection in a pool.
Question	A question may be either a linguistic expression used to make a request for information, or else the request itself made by such an expression. This information is provided with an answer. Questions are normally put forward or asked using interrogative sentences.
First date	A first date is any type of initial meeting between two individuals whether or not previously acquainted where an effort is made to ask, plan and organize some sort of social activity. Dating can vary between cultures, lifestyles, religion, gender, and sexual orientation. In many countries and cultures it is the process that romantic relationships are developed and future spouses are found.
The Gap	The Gap is an ocean cliff, in eastern Sydney, in the state of New South Wales, Australia. It is located in the eastern suburb of Watsons Bay, in the Municipality of Woollahra, near South Head. The Gap is also a suicide location of some notoriety, with a reported 50 suicides annually.

Chapter 7. Listening, Understanding and Supporting Others

Learning	Learning is acquiring new or modifying existing knowledge, behaviors, skills, values, or preferences and may involve synthesizing different types of information. The ability to learn is possessed by humans, animals and some machines. Progress over time tends to follow learning curves.
Agenda	An agenda is a list of meeting activities in the order in which they are to be taken up, by beginning with the call to order and ending with adjournment. It usually includes one or more specific items of business to be dicussed. It may, but is not required to, include specific times for one OR more activities.
Dead Man Walking	Dead Man Walking is a 2002 play written by Tim Robbins based on Dead Man Walking, a book by Sister Helen Prejean about her experiences as a chaplain on death row. Sister Prejean's book has also been made into a film starring Sean Penn and Susan Sarandon. Rather than having it produced professionally, in 2004 he offered the play to schools and colleges throughout the United States, particularly Jesuit schools.
Compter	A compter, was a type of small English prison controlled by a sheriff. The inmates were usually civil prisoners, for example dissenters and debtors. Examples of compters include London's Wood Street Counter, Poultry Compter, Giltspur Street Compter and Borough Compter and the lock-up over the Abbey Gateway, next to St Laurence's church, in Reading, Berkshire (this was the Compter Gate and the lock-up was known as the Compter).
Attack	In computer and computer networks an attack is any attempt to destroy, expose, alter, disable, steal or gain unauthorized access to or make unauthorized use of an asset. Definitions IETF Internet Engineering Task Force defines attack in RFC 2828 as: US Government

91

CNSS Instruction No. 4009 dated 26 April 2010 by Committee on National Security Systems of United States of America defines an attack as:

The increasing dependencies of modern society on information and computers networks (both in private and public sectors, including military) has led to new terms like cyber attack and Cyberwarfare.

CNSS Instruction No. 4009 define a cyber attack as:

Phenomenology

An attack can be active or passive.

An attack can be perpetrated by an insider or from outside the organization;

> An 'inside attack' is an attack initiated by an entity inside the security perimeter (an 'insider'), i.e., an entity that is authorized to access system resources but uses them in a way not approved by those who granted the authorization.
> An 'outside attack' is initiated from outside the perimeter, by an unauthorized or illegitimate user of the system (an 'outsider').

Harassment	Harassment covers a wide range of offensive behaviour. It is commonly understood as behaviour intended to disturb or upset. In the legal sense, it is behaviour which is found threatening or disturbing.
Sexual harassment	Sexual harassment, is intimidation, bullying or coercion of a sexual nature, or the unwelcome or inappropriate promise of rewards in exchange for sexual favors. In some contexts or circumstances, sexual harassment may be illegal. It includes a range of behavior from seemingly mild transgressions and annoyances to actual sexual abuse or sexual assault.

| Advice | Advice is a form of relating personal opinions, belief systems, personal values and recommendations about certain situations relayed in some context to another person, group or party often offered as a guide to action and/or conduct. Put a little more simply, an advice message is a recommendation about what might be thought, said, or otherwise done to address a problem, make a decision, or manage a situation. Advice is believed to be theoretical, and is often considered taboo as well as helpful. |

Chapter 8. Emotions

Space	Space is the boundless, three-dimensional extent in which objects and events occur and have relative position and direction. Physical space is often conceived in three linear dimensions, although modern physicists usually consider it, with time, to be part of the boundless four-dimensional continuum known as spacetime. In mathematics one examines 'spaces' with different numbers of dimensions and with different underlying structures.
Emotional intelligence	Emotional intelligence is an ability, skill or, in the case of the trait Emotional intelligence model, a self-perceived ability to identify, assess, and control the emotions of oneself, of others, and of groups. Various models and definitions have been proposed of which the ability and trait Emotional intelligence models are the most widely accepted in the scientific literature. Criticisms have centered on whether the construct is a real intelligence and whether it has incremental validity over IQ and the Big Five personality dimensions.
Flooding	Flooding is a form of behavior therapy and based on the principles of respondent conditioning. It is sometimes referred to as exposure therapy or Prolonged exposure therapy. As a psychotherapeutic technique, it is used to treat phobia and anxiety disorders including post traumatic stress disorder.
Family	In human context, a family is a group of people affiliated by consanguinity, affinity, or co-residence. In most societies it is the principal institution for the socialization of children. Extended from the human 'family unit' by biological-cultural affinity, marriage, economy, culture, tradition, honor, and friendship are concepts of family that are physical and metaphorical, or that grow increasingly inclusive extending to community, village, city, region, nationhood, global village and humanism.
British American Security Information Council	The British American Security Information Council, is a think tank based in London and Washington, D.C.. It deals with global security issues, such as nuclear policies, armament and disarmament. More recently British American Security Information Council has moved back to a focus making the links between on nuclear non-proliferation and disarmament, specifically on promoting the vision and the steps necessary to achieve a nuclear weapon free world.
Collaboration	Collaboration is a recursive process where two or more people or organizations work together to realize shared goals, -- for example, an intruiging endeavor that is creative in nature--by sharing knowledge, learning and building consensus. Most collaboration requires leadership, although the form of leadership can be social within a decentralized and egalitarian group. In particular, teams that work collaboratively can obtain greater resources, recognition and reward when facing competition for finite resources.

Chapter 8. Emotions

Group	In the social sciences a group can be defined as two or more humans who interact with one another, accept expectations and obligations as members of the group, and share a common identity. By this definition, society can be viewed as a large group, though most social groups are considerably smaller. A true group exhibits some degree of social cohesion and is more than a simple collection or aggregate of individuals, such as people waiting at a bus stop.
Out-group	In sociology, an out-group is a social group towards which an individual feels contempt, opposition, or a desire to compete. Members of outgroups may be subject to outgroup homogeneity biases, and generally people tend to privilege ingroup members over outgroup members in many situations. The term originates from social identity theory.
Convention	A convention, in the sense of a meeting, is a gathering of individuals who meet at an arranged place and time in order to discuss or engage in some common interest. The most common conventions are based upon industry, profession, and fandom. Trade conventions typically focus on a particular industry or industry segment, and feature keynote speakers, vendor displays, and other information and activities of interest to the event organizers and attendees.
Gender	Gender is a set of characteristics distinguishing between male and female, particularly in the cases of men and women. Depending on the context, the discriminating characteristics vary from sex to social role to gender identity. In 1955, sexologist John Money, introduced the terminological distinction between biological sex and gender as a role.
Conflict resolution	Conflict resolution is a range of methods of eliminating sources of conflict. The term 'conflict resolution' is sometimes used interchangeably with the term dispute resolution or alternative dispute resolution. Processes of conflict resolution generally include negotiation, mediation, and diplomacy.
Resolution	A resolution is a written motion adopted by a deliberative body. The substance of the resolution can be anything that can normally be proposed as a motion. For long or important motions, though, it is often better to have them written out so that discussion is easier or so that it can be distributed outside of the body after its adoption.

Chapter 8. Emotions

Emotional contagion	Emotional contagion is the tendency to catch and feel emotions that are similar to and influenced by those of others. One view developed by John Cacioppo of the underlying mechanism is that it represents a tendency to automatically mimic and synchronize facial expressions, vocalizations, postures, and movements with those of another person and, consequently, to converge emotionally. A broader definition of the phenomenon was suggested by Sigal G. Barsade--'a process in which a person or group influences the emotions or behavior of another person or group through the conscious or unconscious induction of emotion states and behavioral attitudes'.
Recall	Recall in memory refers to the retrieval of events or information from the past. Along with encoding and storage, it is one of the three core processes of memory. There are three main types of recall: free recall, cued recall and serial recall.
Self-disclosure	Self-disclosure is both the conscious and unconscious act of revealing more about oneself to others. This may include, but is not limited to, thoughts, feelings, aspirations, goals, failures, successes, fears, dreams as well as one's likes, dislikes, and favorites. Typically, a self-disclosure happens when we initially meet someone and continues as we build and develop our relationships with people.
Language	Language may refer either to the specifically human capacity for acquiring and using complex systems of communication, or to a specific instance of such a system of complex communication. The scientific study of language in any of its senses is called linguistics. The approximately 3000-6000 languages that are spoken by humans today are the most salient examples, but natural languages can also be based on visual rather than auditive stimuli, for example in sign languages and written language.
Favourite	A favourite, was the intimate companion of a ruler or other important person. In medieval and Early Modern Europe, among other times and places, the term is used of individuals delegated significant political power by a ruler. It is especially a phenomenon of the 16th and 17th centuries, when government had become too complex for many hereditary rulers with no great interest or talent for it, and political constitutions were still evolving.

Chapter 8. Emotions

Self-esteem	Self-esteem is a term used in psychology to reflect a person's overall evaluation or appraisal of his or her own worth. Self-esteem encompasses beliefs (for example, 'I am competent', 'I am worthy') and emotions such as triumph, despair, pride and shame. Self-esteem can apply specifically to a particular dimension (for example, 'I believe I am a good writer and I feel happy about that') or have global extent (for example, 'I believe I am a bad person, and feel bad of myself in general').
Fallacy	In logic and rhetoric, a fallacy is incorrect reasoning in argumentation resulting in a misconception. By accident or design, fallacies may exploit emotional triggers in the listener or interlocutor (e.g. appeal to emotion), or take advantage of social relationships between people (e.g. argument from authority). Fallacious arguments are often structured using rhetorical patterns that obscure the logical argument, making fallacies more difficult to diagnose.
Causation	Causation is the 'causal relationship between conduct and result'. That is to say that causation provides a means of connecting conduct with a resulting effect, typically an injury. In criminal law, it is defined as the actus reus (an action) from which the specific injury or other effect arose and is combined with mens rea (a state of mind) to comprise the elements of guilt.
Expectation	In the case of uncertainty, expectation is what is considered the most likely to happen. An expectation, which is a belief that is centered on the future, may or may not be realistic. A less advantageous result gives rise to the emotion of disappointment.
Rumination	Rumination is a way of responding to distress that involves repetitively (and passively) focusing on the symptoms of distress, and on its possible causes and consequences. Rumination is more common in people who are pessimistic, neurotic, and who have negative attributional styles. The tendency to ruminate is a stable constant over time and serves as a significant risk factor for clinical depression.
Computer-mediated communication	Computer-mediated communication is defined as any communicative transaction that occurs through the use of two or more networked computers. While the term has traditionally referred to those communications that occur via computer-mediated formats (e.g., instant messages, e-mails, chat rooms), it has also been applied to other forms of text-based interaction such as text messaging. Research on Computer mediated communication focuses largely on the social effects of different computer-supported communication technologies.

Chapter 9. Dynamics of Interpersonal Relationships

Conflict resolution	Conflict resolution is a range of methods of eliminating sources of conflict. The term 'conflict resolution' is sometimes used interchangeably with the term dispute resolution or alternative dispute resolution. Processes of conflict resolution generally include negotiation, mediation, and diplomacy.
Resolution	A resolution is a written motion adopted by a deliberative body. The substance of the resolution can be anything that can normally be proposed as a motion. For long or important motions, though, it is often better to have them written out so that discussion is easier or so that it can be distributed outside of the body after its adoption.
Thesis	A dissertation or thesis is a document submitted in support of candidature for an academic degree or professional qualification presenting the author's research and findings. In some countries/universities, the word 'thesis' or a cognate is used as part of a bachelor's or master's course, while 'dissertation' is normally applied to a doctorate, whilst, in others, the reverse is true.

The term dissertation can at times be used to describe a treatise without relation to obtaining an academic degree. |
| Language | Language may refer either to the specifically human capacity for acquiring and using complex systems of communication, or to a specific instance of such a system of complex communication. The scientific study of language in any of its senses is called linguistics.

The approximately 3000-6000 languages that are spoken by humans today are the most salient examples, but natural languages can also be based on visual rather than auditive stimuli, for example in sign languages and written language. |
| Fallacy | In logic and rhetoric, a fallacy is incorrect reasoning in argumentation resulting in a misconception. By accident or design, fallacies may exploit emotional triggers in the listener or interlocutor (e.g. appeal to emotion), or take advantage of social relationships between people (e.g. argument from authority). Fallacious arguments are often structured using rhetorical patterns that obscure the logical argument, making fallacies more difficult to diagnose. |

Chapter 9. Dynamics of Interpersonal Relationships

Space	Space is the boundless, three-dimensional extent in which objects and events occur and have relative position and direction. Physical space is often conceived in three linear dimensions, although modern physicists usually consider it, with time, to be part of the boundless four-dimensional continuum known as spacetime. In mathematics one examines 'spaces' with different numbers of dimensions and with different underlying structures.
Reciprocity	In cultural anthropology and sociology, reciprocity is a way of defining people's informal exchange of goods and labour; that is, people's informal economic systems. It is the basis of most non-market economies. Since virtually all humans live in some kind of society and have at least a few possessions, reciprocity is common to every culture.
Computer-mediated communication	Computer-mediated communication is defined as any communicative transaction that occurs through the use of two or more networked computers. While the term has traditionally referred to those communications that occur via computer-mediated formats (e.g., instant messages, e-mails, chat rooms), it has also been applied to other forms of text-based interaction such as text messaging. Research on Computer mediated communication focuses largely on the social effects of different computer-supported communication technologies.
Interpersonal communication	Interpersonal communication is usually defined by communication scholars in numerous ways, usually describing participants who are dependent upon one another and have a shared history. It can involve one on one conversations or individuals interacting with many people within a society. It helps us understand how and why people behave and communicate in different ways to construct and negotiate a social reality.
First date	A first date is any type of initial meeting between two individuals whether or not previously acquainted where an effort is made to ask, plan and organize some sort of social activity. Dating can vary between cultures, lifestyles, religion, gender, and sexual orientation. In many countries and cultures it is the process that romantic relationships are developed and future spouses are found.
Skill	A skill is the learned capacity to carry out pre-determined results often with the minimum outlay of time, energy, or both. Skills can often be divided into domain-general and domain-specific skills. For example, in the domain of work, some general skills would include time management, teamwork and leadership, self motivation and others, whereas domain-specific skills would be useful only for a certain job.

Cram101

Social network	A social network is a social structure made up of individuals (or organizations) called 'nodes', which are tied (connected) by one or more specific types of interdependency, such as friendship, kinship, common interest, financial exchange, dislike, sexual relationships, or relationships of beliefs, knowledge or prestige. Social network analysis views social relationships in terms of network theory consisting of nodes and ties (also called edges, links, or connections). Nodes are the individual actors within the networks, and ties are the relationships between the actors.
Self-disclosure	Self-disclosure is both the conscious and unconscious act of revealing more about oneself to others. This may include, but is not limited to, thoughts, feelings, aspirations, goals, failures, successes, fears, dreams as well as one's likes, dislikes, and favorites. Typically, a self-disclosure happens when we initially meet someone and continues as we build and develop our relationships with people.
Publics	Publics are small groups of people who follow one or more particular issue very closely. They are well informed about the issue(s) and also have a very strong opinion on it/them. They tend to know more about politics than the average person, and, therefore, exert more influence, because these people care so deeply about their cause(s) that they donate much time and money.
Compliance	In psychology, compliance refers to the act of responding favorably to an explicit or implicit request offered by others. The request may be explicit, such as a direct request for donations, or implicit, such as an advertisement promoting its products without directly asking for purchase. In all cases, the target recognizes that he or she is being urged to respond in a desired way.
Punishment	Punishment is the authoritative imposition of something negative or unpleasant on a person or animal in response to behavior deemed wrong by an individual or group. The authority may be either a group or a single person, and punishment may be carried out formally under a system of law or informally in other kinds of social settings such as within a family. Negative consequences that are not authorized or that are administered without a breach of rules are not considered to be punishment as defined here.

Chapter 9. Dynamics of Interpersonal Relationships

Family	In human context, a family is a group of people affiliated by consanguinity, affinity, or co-residence. In most societies it is the principal institution for the socialization of children. Extended from the human 'family unit' by biological-cultural affinity, marriage, economy, culture, tradition, honor, and friendship are concepts of family that are physical and metaphorical, or that grow increasingly inclusive extending to community, village, city, region, nationhood, global village and humanism.
Ethics	Ethics, is a branch of philosophy that addresses questions about morality--that is, concepts such as good and evil, right and wrong, virtue and vice, justice, etc.

Major branches of ethics include:

- Meta-ethics, about the theoretical meaning and reference of moral propositions and how their truth-values (if any) may be determined;
- Normative ethics, about the practical means of determining a moral course of action;
- Applied ethics, about how moral outcomes can be achieved in specific situations;
- Moral psychology, about how moral capacity or moral agency develops and what its nature is;
- Descriptive ethics, about what moral values people actually abide by.

Within each of these branches are many different schools of thought and still further sub-fields of study.

Meta-ethics

Meta-ethics is the branch of ethics that seeks to understand the nature of ethical properties, and ethical statements, attitudes, and judgments.

Chapter 10. Intimacy and Distance in Relationships

Conflict resolution	Conflict resolution is a range of methods of eliminating sources of conflict. The term 'conflict resolution' is sometimes used interchangeably with the term dispute resolution or alternative dispute resolution. Processes of conflict resolution generally include negotiation, mediation, and diplomacy.
Resolution	A resolution is a written motion adopted by a deliberative body. The substance of the resolution can be anything that can normally be proposed as a motion. For long or important motions, though, it is often better to have them written out so that discussion is easier or so that it can be distributed outside of the body after its adoption.
Space	Space is the boundless, three-dimensional extent in which objects and events occur and have relative position and direction. Physical space is often conceived in three linear dimensions, although modern physicists usually consider it, with time, to be part of the boundless four-dimensional continuum known as spacetime. In mathematics one examines 'spaces' with different numbers of dimensions and with different underlying structures.
Computer-mediated communication	Computer-mediated communication is defined as any communicative transaction that occurs through the use of two or more networked computers. While the term has traditionally referred to those communications that occur via computer-mediated formats (e.g., instant messages, e-mails, chat rooms), it has also been applied to other forms of text-based interaction such as text messaging. Research on Computer mediated communication focuses largely on the social effects of different computer-supported communication technologies.
Intellectual	An intellectual is a person who uses intelligence (thought and reason) and critical or analytical reasoning in either a professional or a personal capacity. Terminology and endeavours 'Intellectual' can denote three types of persons: 1. A person involved in, and with, abstract, erudite ideas and theories. 2. A person whose profession (e.g. science, engineering, medicine, literature) solely involves the production and dissemination of ideas. 3. A person of notable cultural and artistic expertise whose knowledge grants him or her intellectual authority in public discourse. Historical perspectives

In English 'intellectual' conveys the general notion of a literate thinker; its earlier usage, such as in The Evolution of an Intellectual by John Middleton Murry, connotes little in the way of 'public' rather than 'literary' activity.

Men of letters

The term 'Man of Letters', has been used in some Western cultures to denote contemporary intellectual men; the term rarely denotes 'scholars', and is not synonymous with 'academic'.

Interpersonal communication	Interpersonal communication is usually defined by communication scholars in numerous ways, usually describing participants who are dependent upon one another and have a shared history. It can involve one on one conversations or individuals interacting with many people within a society. It helps us understand how and why people behave and communicate in different ways to construct and negotiate a social reality.
Self-disclosure	Self-disclosure is both the conscious and unconscious act of revealing more about oneself to others. This may include, but is not limited to, thoughts, feelings, aspirations, goals, failures, successes, fears, dreams as well as one's likes, dislikes, and favorites.
	Typically, a self-disclosure happens when we initially meet someone and continues as we build and develop our relationships with people.
Play	Play refers to a range of voluntary, intrinsically motivated activities that are normally associated with pleasure and enjoyment. Play is commonly associated with children, but Positive psychology has stressed that play is imperative for all higher-functioning animals, even adult humans.
	The rites of play are evident throughout nature and are perceived in people and animals, particularly in the cognitive development and socialization of those engaged in developmental processes and the young.

Cram101

Chapter 10. Intimacy and Distance in Relationships

Withdrawal	A withdrawal is a type of military operation, generally meaning retreating forces back while maintaining contact with the enemy. A withdrawal may be undertaken as part of a general retreat, to consolidate forces, to occupy ground that is more easily defended, or to lead the enemy into an ambush. It is considered a relatively risky operation, requiring discipline to keep from turning into a disorganized rout.
Interaction	In statistics, an interaction may arise when considering the relationship among three or more variables, and describes a situation in which the simultaneous influence of two variables on a third is not additive. Most commonly, interactions are considered in the context of regression analyses. The presence of interactions can have important implications for the interpretation of statistical models.
Group	In the social sciences a group can be defined as two or more humans who interact with one another, accept expectations and obligations as members of the group, and share a common identity. By this definition, society can be viewed as a large group, though most social groups are considerably smaller. A true group exhibits some degree of social cohesion and is more than a simple collection or aggregate of individuals, such as people waiting at a bus stop.
Johari window	A Johari window is a cognitive psychological tool created by Joseph Luft and Harry Ingham in 1955 in the United States, used to help people better understand their interpersonal communication and relationships. It is used primarily in self-help groups and corporate settings as a heuristic exercise. When performing the exercise, subjects are given a list of 56 adjectives and pick five or six that they feel describe their own personality.

117

Chapter 10. Intimacy and Distance in Relationships

Catharsis	Catharsis is a Greek word meaning 'cleansing' or 'purging'. It is derived from the verb καθα?ρειν, kathairein, 'to purify, purge,' and it is related to the adjective καθαρ?ς, katharos, 'pure or clean.' Dramaturgical uses Catharsis is a term in dramatic art that describes the 'emotional cleansing' sometimes depicted in a play as occurring for one or more of its characters, as well as the same phenomenon as (an intended) part of the audience's experience. It describes an extreme change in emotion, occurring as the result of experiencing strong feelings (such as sorrow, fear, pity, or even laughter). It has been described as a 'purification' or a 'purging' of such emotions. More recently, such terms as restoration, renewal, and revitalization have been used when referencing the effect on members of the audience. The Greek philosopher Aristotle was the first to use the term catharsis with reference to the emotions - in his work Poetics. In that context, it refers to a sensation or literary effect that, ideally, would either be experienced by the characters in a play, or be wrought upon the audience at the conclusion of a tragedy; namely, the release of pent-up emotion or energy.
Homosexuality	Homosexuality is romantic and/or sexual attraction or behavior among members of the same sex or gender. As a sexual orientation, homosexuality refers to 'an enduring pattern of or disposition to experience sexual, affectional, or romantic attractions' primarily or exclusively to people of the same sex; 'it also refers to an individual's sense of personal and social identity based on those attractions, behaviors expressing them, and membership in a community of others who share them.' Homosexuality is one of the three main categories of sexual orientation, along with bisexuality and heterosexuality, within the heterosexual-homosexual continuum. The consensus of the behavioral and social sciences and the health and mental health professions is that homosexuality is a normal and positive variation in human sexual orientation, though many religious societies, including Catholicism, Mormonism, and Islam, and some psychological associations, such as NARTH, have traditionally taught that homosexual activity is sinful or dysfunctional.

Chapter 10. Intimacy and Distance in Relationships

Reciprocity	In cultural anthropology and sociology, reciprocity is a way of defining people's informal exchange of goods and labour; that is, people's informal economic systems. It is the basis of most non-market economies. Since virtually all humans live in some kind of society and have at least a few possessions, reciprocity is common to every culture.
Self-defense	Self-defense is a countermeasure that involves defending oneself, one's property or the well-being of another from physical harm. The use of the right of self-defense as a legal justification for the use of force in times of danger is available in many jurisdictions, but the interpretation varies widely. To be acquitted of any kind of physical harm-related crime (such as assault and battery and homicide) using the self-defense justification, one must prove legal provocation, meaning that one must prove that they were in a position where not using self-defense would most likely lead to death, serious injuries and property damage.
Language	Language may refer either to the specifically human capacity for acquiring and using complex systems of communication, or to a specific instance of such a system of complex communication. The scientific study of language in any of its senses is called linguistics. The approximately 3000-6000 languages that are spoken by humans today are the most salient examples, but natural languages can also be based on visual rather than auditive stimuli, for example in sign languages and written language.
Evasion	Evasion is a term used to describe techniques of bypassing an information security device in order to deliver an exploit, attack or other malware to a target network or system, without detection. Evasions are typically used to counter network-based intrusion detection and prevention systems (IPS, IDS) but can also be used to by-pass firewalls. A further target of evasions can be to crash a network security device, rendering it in-effective to subsequent targeted attacks.
Self-assessment	Self-assessment in an organisational setting, according to the EFQM definition, is a comprehensive, systematic and regular review of an organization's activities and results referenced against the EFQM Excellence Model. The self-assessment process allows the organization to discern clearly its strengths and areas in which improvements can be made and culminates in planned improvement actions which are then monitored for progress.

Self-assessment in an educational setting involves students making judgments about their own work.

Go to **Cram101.com** for Interactive Practice Exams for this book or virtually any of your books.
And, **NEVER** highlight a book again!

Chapter 11. Communication Climate

Confirmation	Confirmation is a rite of initiation in Christian churches, normally carried out through the laying on of hands and prayer, and possibly also anointing, for the purpose of bestowing the Gifts of the Holy Spirit. There is an analogous ceremony also called confirmation in Reform Judaism, the most theologically liberal denomination within Judaism. Within Christianity, confirmation is seen as the sealing of the covenant made in Holy Baptism.
Erikson's stages of psychosocial development	Erikson's stages of psychosocial development as articulated by Erik Erikson explain eight stages through which a healthily developing human should pass from infancy to late adulthood. In each stage the person confronts, and hopefully masters, new challenges. Each stage builds on the successful completion of earlier stages.
Space	Space is the boundless, three-dimensional extent in which objects and events occur and have relative position and direction. Physical space is often conceived in three linear dimensions, although modern physicists usually consider it, with time, to be part of the boundless four-dimensional continuum known as spacetime. In mathematics one examines 'spaces' with different numbers of dimensions and with different underlying structures.
Acknowledgment	In the creative arts and scientific literature, an acknowledgment is an expression of gratitude for assistance in creating a literary or artistic work. Receiving credit by way of acknowledgment rather than authorship indicates that the person or organization did not have a direct hand in producing the work in question, but may have contributed funding, criticism, or encouragement to the author(s). Various schemes exist for classifying acknowledgments; Giles ' Councill (2004) give the following six categories: 1. moral support 2. financial support 3. editorial support 4. presentational support 5. instrumental/technical support 6. conceptual support, or peer interactive communication (PIC)

	Apart from citation, which is not usually considered to be an acknowledgment, acknowledgment of conceptual support is widely considered to be the most important for identifying intellectual debt.
Family	In human context, a family is a group of people affiliated by consanguinity, affinity, or co-residence. In most societies it is the principal institution for the socialization of children. Extended from the human 'family unit' by biological-cultural affinity, marriage, economy, culture, tradition, honor, and friendship are concepts of family that are physical and metaphorical, or that grow increasingly inclusive extending to community, village, city, region, nationhood, global village and humanism.
Contempt	Contempt is an intensely negative emotion regarding a person or group of people as inferior, base, or worthless--it is similar to scorn. It is also used when people are being sarcastic. Contempt is also defined as the state of being despised or dishonored; disgrace, and an open disrespect or willful disobedience of the authority of a court of law or legislative body.
Criticism	Criticism is the judgement of the merits and faults of the work or actions of an individual or group by another (the critic). To criticize does not necessarily imply to find fault, but the word is often taken to mean the simple expression of an objection against prejudice, or a disapproval. Another meaning of criticism is the study, evaluation, and interpretation of literature, social movements, film, arts, and similar objects and events.
Forecasting	Forecasting is the process of making statements about events whose actual outcomes (typically) have not yet been observed. A commonplace example might be estimation for some variable of interest at some specified future date. Prediction is a similar, but more general term.
Computer-mediated communication	Computer-mediated communication is defined as any communicative transaction that occurs through the use of two or more networked computers. While the term has traditionally referred to those communications that occur via computer-mediated formats (e.g., instant messages, e-mails, chat rooms), it has also been applied to other forms of text-based interaction such as text messaging. Research on Computer mediated communication focuses largely on the social effects of different computer-supported communication technologies.

Chapter 11. Communication Climate

Interpersonal communication	Interpersonal communication is usually defined by communication scholars in numerous ways, usually describing participants who are dependent upon one another and have a shared history. It can involve one on one conversations or individuals interacting with many people within a society. It helps us understand how and why people behave and communicate in different ways to construct and negotiate a social reality.
Language	Language may refer either to the specifically human capacity for acquiring and using complex systems of communication, or to a specific instance of such a system of complex communication. The scientific study of language in any of its senses is called linguistics. The approximately 3000-6000 languages that are spoken by humans today are the most salient examples, but natural languages can also be based on visual rather than auditive stimuli, for example in sign languages and written language.
Collaboration	Collaboration is a recursive process where two or more people or organizations work together to realize shared goals, -- for example, an intruiging endeavor that is creative in nature--by sharing knowledge, learning and building consensus. Most collaboration requires leadership, although the form of leadership can be social within a decentralized and egalitarian group. In particular, teams that work collaboratively can obtain greater resources, recognition and reward when facing competition for finite resources.
Group	In the social sciences a group can be defined as two or more humans who interact with one another, accept expectations and obligations as members of the group, and share a common identity. By this definition, society can be viewed as a large group, though most social groups are considerably smaller. A true group exhibits some degree of social cohesion and is more than a simple collection or aggregate of individuals, such as people waiting at a bus stop.
Out-group	In sociology, an out-group is a social group towards which an individual feels contempt, opposition, or a desire to compete. Members of outgroups may be subject to outgroup homogeneity biases, and generally people tend to privilege ingroup members over outgroup members in many situations. The term originates from social identity theory.

Chapter 11. Communication Climate

Counterfeit	A counterfeit is an imitation, usually one that is made with the intent of fraudulently passing it off as genuine. Counterfeit products are often produced with the intent to take advantage of the superior value of the imitated product. The word counterfeit frequently describes both the forgeries of currency and documents, as well as the imitations of works of art, clothing, software, pharmaceuticals, watches, electronics and company logos and brands.
Question	A question may be either a linguistic expression used to make a request for information, or else the request itself made by such an expression. This information is provided with an answer. Questions are normally put forward or asked using interrogative sentences.
Neutrality	Neutrality is the absence of declared bias. In an argument, a neutral person will not choose a side. A Neutral country maintains political neutrality, a related but distinct concept.
Respect	Respect denotes both a positive feeling of esteem for a person of other entity (such as a nation or a religion), and also specific actions and conduct representative of that esteem. Respect can be a specific feeling of regard for the actual qualities of the one respected (e.g., 'I have great respect for her judgment'). It can also be conduct in accord with a specific ethic of respect.

Chapter 12. Managing Conflict

Genie	Genie is the pseudonym for a feral child who spent nearly all of the first thirteen years of her life locked inside a bedroom strapped to a potty chair. She was a victim of one of the most severe cases of social isolation in American history. Genie was discovered by Los Angeles authorities on November 4, 1970.
Interaction	In statistics, an interaction may arise when considering the relationship among three or more variables, and describes a situation in which the simultaneous influence of two variables on a third is not additive. Most commonly, interactions are considered in the context of regression analyses.
	The presence of interactions can have important implications for the interpretation of statistical models.
Interdependence	**Interdependence is a dynamic of being mutually and physically responsible to, and sharing a common set of principles with, others. This concept differs distinctly from 'dependence,' which implies that each member of a relationship cannot function or survive apart from one another. In an interdependent relationship, all participants are emotionally, economically, ecologically and/or morally self-reliant while at the same time responsible to each other.**
Language	Language may refer either to the specifically human capacity for acquiring and using complex systems of communication, or to a specific instance of such a system of complex communication. The scientific study of language in any of its senses is called linguistics.
	The approximately 3000-6000 languages that are spoken by humans today are the most salient examples, but natural languages can also be based on visual rather than auditive stimuli, for example in sign languages and written language.
Emperor	An emperor is a (male) monarch, usually the sovereign ruler of an empire or another type of imperial realm. Empress, the female equivalent, may indicate an emperor's wife (empress consort) or a woman who rules in her own right (empress regnant). Emperors are generally recognized to be of a higher honor and rank than kings.

CRAM101

Chapter 12. Managing Conflict

Space	Space is the boundless, three-dimensional extent in which objects and events occur and have relative position and direction. Physical space is often conceived in three linear dimensions, although modern physicists usually consider it, with time, to be part of the boundless four-dimensional continuum known as spacetime. In mathematics one examines 'spaces' with different numbers of dimensions and with different underlying structures.
Opposition	Parliamentary opposition is a form of political opposition to a designated government, particularly in a Westminster-based parliamentary systeme. meaning the administration or the cabinet rather than the state. The title of 'Official Opposition' usually goes to the largest of the parties sitting in opposition with its leader being given the title 'Leader of the Opposition'.
Foresight	In futures studies, especially in Europe, the term 'foresight' has become widely used to describe activities such as: • critical thinking concerning long-term developments, • debate and effort to create wider participatory democracy, • shaping the future, especially by influencing public policy. In the last decade, scenario methods, for example, have become widely used in some European countries in policy-making . The FORSOCIETY network brings together national Foresight teams from most European countries, and the European Foresight Monitoring Project is collating material on Foresight activities around the world. In addition, foresight methods are being used more and more in regional planning and decision -making ('regional foresight').
Collaboration	Collaboration is a recursive process where two or more people or organizations work together to realize shared goals, -- for example, an intruiging endeavor that is creative in nature--by sharing knowledge, learning and building consensus. Most collaboration requires leadership, although the form of leadership can be social within a decentralized and egalitarian group. In particular, teams that work collaboratively can obtain greater resources, recognition and reward when facing competition for finite resources.

Chapter 12. Managing Conflict

Sarcasm	Sarcasm is 'a sharp, bitter, or cutting expression or remark; a bitter jibe or taunt.' Though irony is usually the immediate context, most authorities sharply distinguish sarcasm from irony; however, others argue that sarcasm may or often does involve irony or employs ambivalence. Sarcasm has been suggested as a possible bullying action in some circumstances. Origin of the term It is first recorded in English in 1579, in an annotation to The Shepheardes Calender: October: The word comes from the late Greek σαρκαζμ?ς (sarkazmos) taken from the word σαρκ?ζειν meaning 'to tear flesh, gnash the teeth, speak bitterly'.
Conflict resolution	Conflict resolution is a range of methods of eliminating sources of conflict. The term 'conflict resolution' is sometimes used interchangeably with the term dispute resolution or alternative dispute resolution. Processes of conflict resolution generally include negotiation, mediation, and diplomacy.
Resolution	A resolution is a written motion adopted by a deliberative body. The substance of the resolution can be anything that can normally be proposed as a motion. For long or important motions, though, it is often better to have them written out so that discussion is easier or so that it can be distributed outside of the body after its adoption.
Ritual	A ritual is a set of actions, performed mainly for their symbolic value. It may be prescribed by a religion or by the traditions of a community. The term usually excludes actions which are arbitrarily chosen by the performers.
Friendship	Friendship is a form of interpersonal relationship generally considered to be closer than association, although there is a range of degrees of intimacy in both friendships and associations. Friendship and association can be thought of as spanning across the same continuum. The study of friendship is included in the fields of sociology, social psychology, anthropology, philosophy, and zoology.
Variable	In mathematics, a variable is a value that may change within the scope of a given problem or set of operations. In contrast, a constant is a value that remains unchanged, though often unknown or undetermined. The concepts of constants and variables are fundamental to many areas of mathematics and its applications.

CTam101

Chapter 12. Managing Conflict

Gender	Gender is a set of characteristics distinguishing between male and female, particularly in the cases of men and women. Depending on the context, the discriminating characteristics vary from sex to social role to gender identity. In 1955, sexologist John Money, introduced the terminological distinction between biological sex and gender as a role.
Brainstorming	Brainstorming is a group creativity technique designed to generate a large number of ideas for the solution of a problem. In 1953 the method was popularized by Alex Faickney Osborn in a book called Applied Imagination. Osborn proposed that groups could double their creative output with brainstorming.
Reciprocity	In cultural anthropology and sociology, reciprocity is a way of defining people's informal exchange of goods and labour; that is, people's informal economic systems. It is the basis of most non-market economies. Since virtually all humans live in some kind of society and have at least a few possessions, reciprocity is common to every culture.
Respect	Respect denotes both a positive feeling of esteem for a person of other entity (such as a nation or a religion), and also specific actions and conduct representative of that esteem. Respect can be a specific feeling of regard for the actual qualities of the one respected (e.g., 'I have great respect for her judgment'). It can also be conduct in accord with a specific ethic of respect.
Structuring	Structuring, is the practice of executing financial transactions (such as the making of bank deposits) in a specific pattern calculated to avoid the creation of certain records and reports required by law, such as the United States's Bank Secrecy Act (BSA) and Internal Revenue Code section 6050I . Legal restrictions on structuring can have some of the same economic effects as capital controls in some economies, as the restrictions effectively limit the flow of capital by magnitude and duration. Structuring controls can apply equally to taking money out of a nation as well as putting money into the finance system in a nation.
Sibling	Siblings (also called sibs) are people who share at least one parent. A male sibling is called a brother; and a female sibling is called a sister. In most societies throughout the world, siblings usually grow up together and spend a good deal of their childhood socializing with one another.

Chapter 12. Managing Conflict

Social support	Social support is the physical and emotional comfort given to us by our family, friends, co-workers and others. It is knowing that we are part of a community of people who love and care for us, and value and think well of us. Social support is a way of categorizing the rewards of communication in a particular circumstance.
Element	Under United States law, an element of a crime or element of an offense is one of the various facts (collectively, the elements of the offense) whose proof in the conjunctive (i.e., all of whose proof) is a necessary condition for legal proof that a defendant has committed a given crime. (Some elements are phrased in the disjunctive, such that an element may be proven by proving any of multiple facts, but in such a situation the easy fact '[fact A] or [fact B] ... or [fact n]' becomes the element whose proof is among the necessary conditions for proof of the offense). Before a court finds a defendant guilty of a criminal offense, the prosecution must present evidence that, even when opposed by any evidence the defense may choose to present, is credible and sufficient to prove beyond a reasonable doubt that the defendant committed each element of the particular crime charged.
Environment	The biophysical environment is the symbiosis between the physical environment and the biological life forms within the environment, and includes all variables that comprise the Earth's biosphere. The biophysical environment can be divided into two categories: the natural environment and the built environment, with some overlap between the two. Following the industrial revolution, the built environment has become an increasingly significant part of the Earth's environment.
Family	In human context, a family is a group of people affiliated by consanguinity, affinity, or co-residence. In most societies it is the principal institution for the socialization of children. Extended from the human 'family unit' by biological-cultural affinity, marriage, economy, culture, tradition, honor, and friendship are concepts of family that are physical and metaphorical, or that grow increasingly inclusive extending to community, village, city, region, nationhood, global village and humanism.
Alcoholism	Alcoholism is a disabling addictive disorder. It is characterized by compulsive and uncontrolled consumption of alcohol despite its negative effects on the drinker's health, relationships, and social standing. Like other drug addictions, alcoholism is medically defined as a treatable disease.
Child Life	Child Life is a discipline that relates to the study of stages of a child's development. Child Life specialists require a bachelors degree or masters degree offered by many colleges.

141

Chapter 12. Managing Conflict

	Child Life Specialists primarily work in hospital settings.
Narrative	A narrative is a story that is created in a constructive format (as a work of speech, writing, song, film, television, video games, photography or theatre) that describes a sequence of fictional or non-fictional events. Ultimately its origin is found in the Proto-Indo-European root gno-, 'to know'.

The word 'story' may be used as a synonym of 'narrative', but can also be used to refer to the sequence of events described in a narrative. |
| Origin | Origin is a scientific graphing and data analysis software package, produced by OriginLab Corporation, that runs on Microsoft Windows. Origin supports various 2D/3D graph types.

Data analyses in Origin include statistics, signal processing, curve fitting and peak analysis. |
Attitude	An attitude is a hypothetical construct that represents an individual's degree of like or dislike for something. Attitudes are generally positive or negative views of a person, place, thing, or event-- this is often referred to as the attitude object. People can also be conflicted or ambivalent toward an object, meaning that they simultaneously possess both positive and negative attitudes toward the item in question.
Conformity	Conformity is the act of matching attitudes, beliefs, and behaviors to what individuals perceive is normal of their society or social group. This influence occurs in small groups and society as a whole, and may result from subtle unconscious influences, or direct and overt social pressure. Conformity can occur in the presence of others, or when an individual is alone.
Conversation	Conversation is interactive, more-or-less spontaneous, communication between two or more conversants. Interactivity occurs because contributions to a conversation are response reactions to what has previously been said. Spontaneity occurs because a conversation must proceed, to some extent, and in some way, unpredictably.

Chapter 12. Managing Conflict

Laissez-faire	In economics, laissez-faire describes an environment in which transactions between private parties are free from state intervention, including restrictive regulations, taxes, tariffs and enforced monopolies.
	The phrase laissez-faire is French and literally means 'let do', but it broadly implies 'let it be', or 'leave it alone.'
	Origins of the phrase
	According to historical legend, the phrase stems from a meeting in about 1680 between the powerful French finance minister Jean-Baptiste Colbert and a group of French businessmen led by a certain M. Le Gendre. When the eager mercantilist minister asked how the French state could be of service to the merchants and help promote their commerce, Le Gendre replied simply 'Laissez-nous faire' ('Leave us be', lit.
Computer-mediated communication	Computer-mediated communication is defined as any communicative transaction that occurs through the use of two or more networked computers. While the term has traditionally referred to those communications that occur via computer-mediated formats (e.g., instant messages, e-mails, chat rooms), it has also been applied to other forms of text-based interaction such as text messaging. Research on Computer mediated communication focuses largely on the social effects of different computer-supported communication technologies.
Conflict management	Conflict management involves implementing strategies to limit the negative aspects of conflict and to increase the positive aspects of conflict at a level equal to or higher than where the conflict is taking place. Furthermore, the aim of conflict management is to enhance learning and group outcomes (effectiveness or performance in organizational setting) (Rahim, 2002, p. 208). It is not concerned with eliminating all conflict or avoiding conflict.
Interpersonal communication	Interpersonal communication is usually defined by communication scholars in numerous ways, usually describing participants who are dependent upon one another and have a shared history. It can involve one on one conversations or individuals interacting with many people within a society. It helps us understand how and why people behave and communicate in different ways to construct and negotiate a social reality.

Clam101

Chapter 12. Managing Conflict

Power	In physics, power is the rate at which work is performed or energy is converted As a simple example, if an elevated reservoir is used to drive a waterwheel, then replacing its drain valve with another of larger diameter does not change the water's potential energy, but does increase the available power because the larger valve allows higher flow, so the potential energy can be more quickly converted into kinetic energy.

If ΔW is the amount of work performed during a period of time of duration Δt, the average power P_{avg} over that period is given by the formula

$$P_{avg} = \frac{\Delta W}{\Delta t} .$$

It is the average amount of work done or energy converted per unit of time. The average power is often simply called 'power' when the context makes it clear.

Work	In physics, mechanical work is the amount of energy transferred by a force acting through a distance. Like energy, it is a scalar quantity, with SI units of joules. The term work was first coined in 1826 by the French mathematician Gaspard-Gustave Coriolis.
Publics	Publics are small groups of people who follow one or more particular issue very closely. They are well informed about the issue(s) and also have a very strong opinion on it/them. They tend to know more about politics than the average person, and, therefore, exert more influence, because these people care so deeply about their cause(s) that they donate much time and money.
Group	In the social sciences a group can be defined as two or more humans who interact with one another, accept expectations and obligations as members of the group, and share a common identity. By this definition, society can be viewed as a large group, though most social groups are considerably smaller.

A true group exhibits some degree of social cohesion and is more than a simple collection or aggregate of individuals, such as people waiting at a bus stop.

Chapter 12. Managing Conflict

Team	A team comprises a group of people or animals linked in a common purpose. Teams are especially appropriate for conducting tasks that are high in complexity and have many interdependent subtasks. A group in itself does not necessarily constitute a team.
Reinforcement	Reinforcement is a term in operant conditioning and behavior analysis for the process of increasing the rate or probability of a behavior (e.g. pulling a lever more frequently) by the delivery or emergence of a stimulus (e.g. a candy) immediately or shortly after the behavior, called a 'response,' is performed. The response strength is assessed by measuring frequency, duration, latency, accuracy, and/or persistence of the response after reinforcement stops. Experimental behavior analysts measured the rate of responses as a primary demonstration of learning and performance in non-humans (e.g. the number of times a pigeon pecks a key in a 10-minute session).
Skill	A skill is the learned capacity to carry out pre-determined results often with the minimum outlay of time, energy, or both. Skills can often be divided into domain-general and domain-specific skills. For example, in the domain of work, some general skills would include time management, teamwork and leadership, self motivation and others, whereas domain-specific skills would be useful only for a certain job.
Distribution	Product distribution is one of the four elements of the marketing mix. An organization or set of organizations (go-betweens) involved in the process of making a product or service available for use or consumption by a consumer or business user. The other three parts of the marketing mix are product, pricing, and promotion.
Referent power	Referent power is individual power based on a high level of identification with, admiration of, or respect for the powerholder.

Chapter 12. Managing Conflict

Nationalism, patriotism, celebrities and well-respected people are examples of referent power in effect.

Referent power is one of the Five Bases of Social Power, as defined by Bertram Raven and his colleagues in 1959.

Job interview

A job interview is a process in which a potential employee is evaluated by an employer for prospective employment in their company, organization, or firm. During this process, the employer hopes to determine whether or not the applicant is suitable for the job.

Role

A job interview typically precedes the hiring decision, and is used to evaluate the candidate.

Lightning Source UK Ltd.
Milton Keynes UK
UKHW031411110919
349550UK00002B/10/P

9 781428 866348